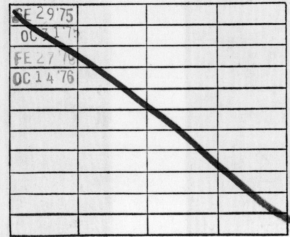

Twayne's United States Authors Series

Sylvia E. Bowman, *Editor*

INDIANA UNIVERSITY

John Dewey

JOHN DEWEY

By HARRY M. CAMPBELL

Oklahoma State University

 189

Twayne Publishers, Inc.   ::   New York

To My Wife

Preface

THIS STUDY of John Dewey concentrates on the period (beginning in 1925 with *Experience and Nature*) in which his most important books were published. Except for less emphasis on the pedagogical aspects of education, these books are mainly concerned with the same general problems treated in his works after Dewey abandoned his early devotion to Christianity and Hegel; but, perhaps because he spent more time in writing and less in espousing causes, in his major phase he develops, clarifies, and occasionally modifies his views on such basic problems as nature, logic, religion, knowledge and freedom. In these books Dewey also has time to defend himself in detail against attacks evoked especially by his *Studies in Logical Theory* (1903) and other works, and, in turn, to launch sharp attacks against his critics. The embattled Dewey writes usually with animation and with forcefulness when his style is not marred, as it too often is, by ambiguity and verbosity. In his major books his attacks on opposing positions are usually made without naming his opponents, but he had to mention names in his replies to critics in the Schilpp volume (in the Library of Living Philosophers), and he chose to do so in numerous articles, especially as he grew older and (at least in print) more irritable. In fact, he did not hesitate, for example, to name and to attack sharply several of the logical empiricists who considered themselves his allies.

The introductory chapter gives a brief biographical sketch of Dewey, including an account of his early attempt to combine Christianity and Hegelianism, and his abandonment of this attempt about 1890 in favor of a naturalism which retained some traces of Hegelianism but which resulted in very intemperate attacks on Christianity. Chapter 2 studies typical and important articles written soon after his break with Christianity and Hegelianism, and it concludes with a brief treatment of *Democracy and Education* (1916), his most important book before *Experience and Nature* (1925). Chapters 3 through 7 discuss the development of his experimental naturalism, which gradually became more and more mingled with a buoyant romanticism. Under the inspiration of this romantic vision, Dewey prophesied in extravagant terms a scientific-esthetic millennium when the panacea of the scientific method would be universally and spontaneously effective not only in material science but with the same precision in morals and naturalistic religion as well. Chapter 8 compares Dewey with some of his outstanding contemporaries, and Chapter 9 gives a final evaluation, with which his devoted followers will disagree but which I believe they will find challenging.

In conclusion, I should express appreciation for helpful suggestions and information to three people associated with the Center for Co-operative Research on Dewey Publications at Southern Illinois University: Professor George E. Axtelle, Director; Mrs. Joanna Boydston, Editor; and Professor George S. Counts. For a reduction in teaching load enabling me to do the research that eventually resulted in this book, I am grateful to the Research Foundation of Oklahoma State University. Most of all, I am indebted to the very patient and distinguished Editor of the Twayne United States Author Series, Dr. Sylvia Bowman, whose suggestions for the improvement of this book have been invaluable.

HARRY M. CAMPBELL

Oklahoma State University
Stillwater

Contents

Chronology

1859   John Dewey born, Burlington, Vermont, October 20.

1879   Graduated from University of Vermont.

1879-   Teacher in secondary schools.
1882

1882-   Graduate studies at John Hopkins University; doctoral
1884   degree, 1884.

1884-   Instructor in Philosophy, University of Michigan.
1888

1886   Marriage to Alice Chipman.

1888-   Professor of Philosophy, University of Minnesota.
1889

1889   *The School and Society* published (revised edition, 1915).

1894   Chairman of the Department of Philosophy, Psychology, and Pedagogy, University of Chicago.

1896   Founder of the Laboratory School.

1899   President of the American Psychological Association.

1903   *Studies in Logical Theory* published.

1904-   Professor of Philosophy, Columbia University. Also teaching
1930   at Teachers College, Columbia University.

1905   President of the Eastern division of the American Philosophical Association.

1908   *Ethics*, with James H. Tufts published (revised edition, 1932).

1910   *How We Think* (revised edition, 1933) and *The Influence of Darwin on Philosophy* published.

1915   First president and one of founders of American Association of University Professors.

1916   Co-founder of the original teacher-union movement in New York City; later a charter member of the New York Teachers Guide, American Federation of Teachers; *Democracy and Education* and *Essays in Experimental Logic* published.

1919   Visits Japan; lectures at Tokyo Imperial University.

1919-   Visits in China; lectures at national universities in Peking and
1921   Nanking.

1920   *Reconstruction in Philosophy* published (enlarged edition, 1948).

1922   *Human Nature and Conduct* published (Modern Library edition, 1930).

1923   Delivers first series of Carus Lectures before meeting of American Philosophical Association at Columbia University.

1925   *Experience and Nature* published (revised edition, 1929).

1927   Death of Alice Chipman Dewey; *The Public and Its Problems* published.

1929   President of the Peoples Lobby and chairman of the League for Independent Political Action; delivers Gifford Lectures at Edinburgh; *Characters and Events* (edited by Joseph Ratner) and *The Quest for Certainty* published.

1930-   Professor emeritus at Columbia University.
1952

1930   *Individualism, Old and New* published.

1931   Delivers William James Lectures at Harvard University; *Philosophy and Civilization* published.

1934   Delivers Terry Lectures at Yale University; *Art as Experience* and *A Common Faith* published.

1935   *Liberalism and Social Action* published.

1937   Chairman of the Commission of Inquiry into the Charges against Leon Trotsky.

1938   *Logic: The Theory of Inquiry* published.

1939   *Freedom and Culture* published.

1946   *Problems of Men* published; marriage to Roberta L. Grant.

1949   *Knowing and the Known* (with Arthur F. Bentley) published.

1952   Died, June 1.

CHAPTER 1

Biography and Introduction

J OHN DEWEY was born in Burlington, Vermont, October 20, 1859. He attended the public schools there, graduating from high school at the age of fifteen. As a bookish lad, he was bored by the routine, unimaginative method in which classes were conducted. At the University of Vermont, which he attended from 1875 to 1879, he developed an interest in physiology, psychology, and (especially) philosophy. He was greatly influenced by his philosophy teacher, Professor H. A. P. Torrey, who directed his studies in this subject not only at the university but for three years afterward, and who first, says Dewey, "turned my thoughts definitely to the study of philosophy as a life pursuit . . . ."[1]

After graduating in 1879, Dewey taught in secondary schools, for three years, the first two at a high school in the small town of Oil City, Pennsylvania. While he was teaching there, he had a religious experience which influenced him for the rest of his life but which was not recorded until, at the age of eighty-two, he talked about it to Max Eastman in an interview. As Eastman records Dewey's statement in his article in *The Atlantic Monthly*,

> One evening while he sat reading he had what he calls a "mystical experience." It was an answer to that question which still worried him: whether he really meant business when he prayed . . . . There was no vision, not even a definable emotion—just a supremely blissful feeling that his worries were over. Mystical experience in general, Dewey explains, are purely emotional and cannot be conveyed in words. But when he tries to convey his in words, it comes out like this:—
>
> "What the hell are you worrying about, anyway? Everything that's here is here, and you can just lie back on it."
>
> "I've never had any doubts since then," he adds, "nor any beliefs. To me faith means not worrying."

Although his religion has so little affirmative content,—and has nothing to do, he is sure, with his philosophy,—Dewey likens it to the *poetic pantheism* [italics mine] of Wordsworth, whom he was reading at that time, and to Walt Whitman's sense of oneness with the universe. To forestall your own remark, he reminds you that it is very likely a sublimation of sex, and points out that this doesn't make it any less normal or important.

"I claim I've got religion," he concludes, "and that I got it that night in Oil City."[2]

As a result of his intensive reading in philosophy, Dewey had two articles—"The Metaphysical Assumptions of Materialism" and "The Pantheism of Spinoza"—published in 1882 in *The Journal of Speculative Philosophy*, of which William T. Harris was the editor.

I *Hegelian and Christian Influence*

From 1882 to 1884, Dewey did graduate work in philosophy at John Hopkins University and completed his doctorate. He studied psychology under G. Stanley Hall and some philosophy under Charles Sanders Peirce, but his favorite teacher was George Sylvester Morris, under whose influence he developed a deep interest in Hegel. Dewey tried to combine Hegel's doctrine of an immanent world consciousness with his own belief at this time in a Christian God. Dewey followed Hegel in positing a transcendent Absolute Idea (or immanent world consciousness) which manifested itself in the world of experience and which unified all experience in an evolving universe. As late as 1884 Dewey considered it a sin not to believe in God; but, after he became interested in Hegel, he decided that the Christian view of God as a kind of person could better be explained as this all-unifying Absolute Idea or World Spirit.

As Dewey says in his autobiographical essay, "From Absolutism to Experimentalism," "Hegel's synthesis of subject and object, matter and spirit, the divine and the human, was. . . . no mere intellectual formula; it operated as an immense release, a liberation. Hegel's treatment of human culture, of institutions and the arts, involved the same dissolution of hard-and-fast dividing walls, and had a special attraction for me."[3] What Dewey means by Hegel's ‹synthesis is that Hegel, unlike Kant, did not believe that thought exists apart from fact; the two must be arbitrarily joined. As Dewey said in an article of this period published in the *Monist*: "When Hegel calls thought objective he means just what he says: that there is no special, apart faculty of thought belonging to and operated by a mind existing separate from the outer world. What Hegel means by objective thought is the meaning, the significance of the fact itself; and by methods of thought he understands simply the processes in which meaning of this fact is involved."[4] In his conception of reality as a connected system or an organic unity, Hegel, in Dewey's opinion, anticipated the scientific outlook, which was becoming more and more important to Dewey.

Although in the autobiographical sketch "From Absolutism to Experimentalism" Dewey refers at some length to the influence of Hegel on him and even acknowledges that this influence "left a permanent deposit in his thinking," he makes no reference in this essay to his youthful adherence to Christianity. However, his adherence to both these forms of transcendence is evident in his articles published during the first part of the decade from 1884 to 1894, when he was teaching at the University of Michigan (except for one year when he was visiting professor at the University of Minnesota). Although his God at this time was, from one point of view (as we have seen), the neo-Hegelian universal consciousness or spirit, "an ideal unity of purpose and meaning," he also believed in the God of the Bible. Dewey insisted, in an address to a group of Christian students at Ann Arbor in late 1884, that refusal to believe in God "is definitely a moral lapse, a sin." As Father John Blewett says of this address, later published as an article entitled "The Obligation to Knowledge of God," "Conceding that the sober witness of the Bible to the reality of God and His claims on man strikes the unregenerate as hard doctrine, the young professor argued that the truth of this Biblical teaching comes home to one only when 'the commands it lays upon the will have been executed.' "[5]

II *The "Permanent Deposit"*

The rather incongruous association of Hegelianism and Christianity described above did not last very long in Dewey's restless thinking. About the middle of the decade at Ann Arbor he rather suddenly dropped Christianity, and for the rest of his life he remained vehemently anti-Christian. This change was no doubt accentuated by his marriage in 1886 to Alice Chapman, who felt "that a religious attitude was indigenous in natural experience and that theology and ecclesiastic institutions had benumbed rather than promoted it."[6] His abandonment of Hegelianism was more gradual and traces of it remained permanently in his thinking. The "permanent deposit" left by Hegelianism was its emphasis on the organic unity of all existence. Under the unfluence of William James and Darwin, as we shall see later, Dewey gave this unity a biological emphasis not present in Hegel's transcendent World Consciousness.

For Hegel, adjustment, as Morton White says, "meant that the universe was in some sense constituted by thought before any human mind began to think. On the other hand, the force of Darwin's analysis was to portray man and his distinctive capacity—thought—as a product of certain natural forces of adjustment. Adjustment did not mean the reinstatement of some previously existing harmony, and therefore thought was not the deciphering of riddles already solved by an Absolute that kept the answers secret. Thought was an active transformation of a situation, and introduced a new element."[7] Such was the kind of reasoning that led Dewey gradually away from Hegel's universal mind.

III *Educator and Writer*

In 1894 Dewey went to the University of Chicago as chairman of the Department of Philosophy, Psychology, and Pedagogy; and he remained there until 1904. In 1896 he founded the Laboratory School for elementary pupils, which was to have a great and lasting influence on American education. His book *School and Society* (1900) was developed from talks given to raise money for this school. Because of his interest in making schools an illustration of, rather than a mere preparation for, democracy in action, Dewey worked with many famous educators whose ideas on education were similar to his, and among these personages was Jane Addams at Hull House. During his decade at Chicago, besides his teaching there and lecturing at various other places, Dewey was busy publishing and inspiring his graduate students to publish. One result was the volume entitled *Studies in Logical Theory* (1903), which consists of essays by graduate students with a long introductory essay by Dewey. This book, which seemed to reinforce William James's pragmatism, was praised by James, although it was condemned by most other readers.

If we may judge from Dewey's hostile attitude in print throughout his life toward those who disagreed with him, it is not surprising that there was friction between him and the president of the University of Chicago about the administration of the Laboratory School. The evidence, however, seems to indicate that Dewey was in the right; and he seems to have been justified in resigning in 1904. Although Dewey had no other position when he resigned, he was appointed professor of philosophy at Columbia University that same fall and remained there until he retired and was made professor emeritus in 1930. Besides his teaching at Columbia and his lecturing at various other places, usually under the auspices of some important foundation, Dewey's publication of both books and articles became increasingly voluminous and did not diminish markedly until after he was ninety years old. The most important of his many books published after he went to Columbia are listed in the Selected Bibliography at the end of this study.

Several of these books consisted of lectures given under the auspices of the foundations mentioned above; a few were collections of essays that had appeared before in periodicals; most of them were a development of books previously published. For example, Dewey begins the Preface of *Logic: The Theory of Inquiry* (1938) by saying: "This book is a development of ideas regarding the nature of logical theory that were first presented, some forty years ago, in *Studies in Logical Theory*; that were somewhat expanded in *Essays in Experimental Logic* and were briefly summarized with special reference to education in *How We Think*."[8]

Indeed, this procedure is characteristic of most of the books written in what Professor Richard Bernstein calls the third phase of Dewey's philosophic development, beginning with the publication of *Experience and Nature* in 1925. As Professor Bernstein says of this last period, "this is Dewey's most interesting and important period. He returns to earlier ideas, re-examines them, and critically analyzes the presuppositions of his position. Interrelations among the various aspects of his philosophy are made more explicit, and there is the emergence of a coherent and comprehensive point of view."[9]

It must not be forgotten, however, that Dewey did far more than

17

lecture and write numerous books and articles after he went to Columbia in 1904. He was active in various movements promoting democracy, which had become so important to him that one critic has called it his "religion."[10] Indeed, his daughter's biography contains this statement: "In his earlier years Dewey shared the faith then rather common that American democracy in its normal evolution would in time do away with the serious injustices of the economic field."[11]

Among Dewey's outside activities after he went to Columbia may be mentioned the following: In 1905, he became president of the Eastern division of the American Philosophical Association. In 1915, he was one of the founders and the first president of the American Association of University Professors. In 1916, he was one of the founders of the original teacher-union movement in New York City, and he later became a charter member of the New York Guild of the American Federation of Teachers. In 1919, he visited Japan and gave a series of lectures (later published in the volume entitled *Reconstruction in Philosophy*) at Tokyo Imperial University.

From 1919 to 1921, he visited extensively in China and lectured at national universities at Peking and Nanking. As Miss Jane Dewey says, "His visits to Turkey in 1924 and to Mexico in 1926 confirmed his belief in the power and necessity of education to secure revolutionary changes to the benefit of the individual, so that they cannot become mere alterations in the external form of a nation's culture."[12] In 1928, Dewey visited Russia and was so favorably impressed with the educational system there that, as Miss Jane Dewey says, "he wrote a series of articles very sympathetic with the U.S.S.R., which led to his being described as a 'Bolshevik' and a 'red' in the conservative press."[13] Needless to say, later events in Russia made him change his views and condemn Soviet totalitarianism.

In 1921, Dewey became president of the Peoples Lobby and chairman of the League for Independent Political Action; and, in the same year, he delivered the Gifford Lectures at Edinburgh (later published in the volume entitled *Quest for Certainty*). In 1937, he served as a member of the Commission of Inquiry into the charges against Leon Trotsky; and, after careful and scholarly investigation, he joined the other members of the commission in finding Trotsky not guilty. As Miss Jane Dewey says, "In left wing circles he was now denounced indifferently as a Trotskyite or as a reactionary and a section of the conservative press welcomed him into a fold in which he has never belonged."[14] Miss Dewey says, no doubt correctly, that all her father's political activities were prompted by "liberalism" in the most truly democratic sense of that widely misunderstood term.

To conclude this brief biographical sketch of Dewey's life, it should be mentioned that Dewey and his first wife, Alice Chapman Dewey (who died in 1927), had six children of their own, two of whom, Morris and Gordon, died at an early age. They adopted one Italian boy, Sabino, while they were on a trip to Italy. The oldest daughter, Evelyn, and Sabino both became distinguished educators. Both Evelyn and Frederick, a son who lived to adulthood, are deceased; but Sabino is still active. Dr. Jane Dewey, now working at Aberdeen Proving Grounds, Aberdeen, Maryland, is a distinguished physicist. Another daughter, Mrs. Lucy Brandauer Wolf, now resides at Havre de Grace, Maryland. In 1946 Dewey married Roberta L. Grant, and they adopted two children, John, Jr., and Adrienne. Dewey died on June 1, 1952, at the age of ninety-two. The second Mrs. Dewey now lives in New York City.[15]

CHAPTER 2

The Early and Middle Years: Developing a Philosophy of Experimental Naturalism

I   *The Individual and Science: "A New Heaven and a New Earth"*

SINCE enough has been said in Chapter I about Dewey's early Hegelianized Christianity, it will be sufficient to begin this chapter with his statement that, between 1885 and 1900, he "drifted away from Hegelianism." Although Dewey never mentions his early adherence to any form of Christianity, it is apparent that in the mid-1880's he radically revolted from it; and, as Father John Blewett aptly states in his careful study of Dewey's early writings, "between 1891 and 1894 Dewey became a Saul of Tarsus in reverse. If a dedicated person is a religious person—a possible use of a notoriously nebulous word—then American history has known few such religious men as John Dewey."[1]

In examining some of his early works as preliminary sketches for the important books of his last period, it is appropriate to begin with an essay written in 1897, "The Significance of the Problem of Knowledge."[2] In this essay, individual man, in the interchange between man and nature which is always fundamental in Dewey's naturalism, seems to be the senior partner. The theme is the liberation of the individual, beginning with the Renaissance, from the authoritarian control of the Middle Ages. Dewey does not blame the Middle Ages for such control; it is almost as if the emphasis in each period were part of a great overruling plan of some force like Hegel's World Spirit. If such an emphasis had been called to his attention, Dewey would no doubt have explained it in evolutionary terms as a mere adjustment to environment. At any rate, he rather graciously gives credit for fulfilling a role to "medieval civilization," which "knew that the time had not come when these appetites and impulses of the individual could be trusted to work" but had to "be controlled by the incorporate truths inherited from Athens and Rome." Happily, however, "just because the authoritative truth of medievalism has succeeded, has fulfilled its function, the individual beginning with the Renaissance can begin to assert himself."[3] Then follows a passage in which Dewey's evangelical fervor and Romantic prophesying (increasingly evident in the later books) already begin to appear:

Hence the conception of progress as a ruling idea; the conception of the individual as the source and standard of rights; and the problem of knowledge, were all born together. Given the freed individual, who feels called upon to create a new heaven and a new earth, and who feels himself gifted with the power to perform the task to which he is called: —and the demand for science, for a method of discovering and verifying truth, becomes imperious. The individual is henceforth to supply control, law, and not simply stimulation and initiation.[4]

In this early essay of 1897 Dewey is more tolerant than he is later of philosophies that differ from his, perhaps because the rather large volume of adverse criticism that followed his contributions to *Studies in Logical Theory* (1903) had not begun to appear. Nonetheless, Dewey makes it quite clear that his own philosophy is superior to that of the others, who have "played their part" or "served their time":

The sensationalist has played his part in bringing to effective recognition the demand in valid knowledge for individuality of experience, for personal participation in materials of knowledge. The rationalist has served his time in making it clear once for all that valid knowledge requires organization, and the operation of a relatively permanent and general factor. The Kantian epistemologist has formulated the claims of both schools in defining judgment as the relation of perception and conception. But when it goes on to state that this relation is itself knowledge, or can be found in knowledge, it stultifies itself. Knowledge can define the percept and elaborate the concept, but their union can be found only in action. The experimental method of modern science, its erection into the ultimate mode of verification, is simply this fact obtaining recognition.[5]

What Dewey says about knowledge as action and about the scientific method is essentially what he says for the rest of his long life.

He also evinces the same interest that he is to maintain in "the growing transfer of interest from metaphysics and the theory of knowledge to psychology and social ethics—including in the latter term all the related concrete social sciences, so far as they may give guidance to conduct."[6] The psychology was one with a biological emphasis (as he had found it in one aspect of William James's *Principles of Psychology*) so that the old mind-body dualism could be avoided.

In other words, mind and body were not two separate entities miraculously brought together by divine intervention, but human life developed gradually from lower forms in what Dewey called "the biological matrix," and, at a certain stage of complexity, what we call "mind" appeared. In *Experience and Nature*, he explains more fully: "As life is a character of events in a peculiar condition of organization, and 'feeling' is a quality of life-forms marked by complexly mobile and discrimination responses, so 'mind' is an added property assumed by a feeling creature, when it reaches the organized interaction with other living creatures which is language communication. . . . The distinction between physical, psychophysical, and mental is thus one of levels of increasing complexity and intimacy of interaction among natural events."[7]

II   *Nature Leads the Way:*
"Things Come When They Are Wanted"

If Dewey seems to stress the individual more than nature in this 1897 essay, he makes amends to nature in an essay entitled "'Consciousness' and Experience"[8] that appeared in 1899 and was reprinted in 1910 in *The Influence of Darwin on Philosophy*. In the later essay, nature cooperates with the individual to correct the errors of the analytic school of psychology with its "elementary contents and external associations," as well as those of the intellectualistic school "with its pure self-consciousness as a source of ultimate truths, its hierarchy of intuitions, its ready-made faculties."[9] Both nature and man work together here in a "unity of function" that produces "movement in growth" and that helps to remove the dualistic error which supposes "that values are externally obtruded [or handed down by a transcendent God] and statically set in irrelevant rubbish." The part that nature plays, since it is so much like that later developed in *Experience and Nature*, is worth quoting in full:

> Nothing is more naive than to suppose that in pursuing "natural history" (term of scorn in which yet resides the dignity of the world-drama) we simply learn something of the temporal conditions under which a given value appears, while its own eternal essential quality remains as opaque as before. Nature *knows* no such divorce of quality and circumstance. Things come *when they are wanted* and *as they are wanted*; their quality is *precisely* the *response they give to the conditions that call for them*, while the furtherance they afford to the movement of their whole is their meaning. [italics mine][10]

All the ignorance of those who believe in a transcendent God will be eliminated (it is implied) if they simply learn that nature "knows"; and, so it almost seems, nature arranges (or at least co-operates in) evolution so that "Things come when they are wanted and as they are wanted" and give the proper "response . . . to the conditions that call for them . . . ."

III *Man the Benefactor of Nature*

If nature seems to take the initiative in this 1899 essay, Dewey has by 1905 (in "Beliefs and Existences,"[11] reprinted in *The Influence of Darwin on Philosophy)* restored the more important role to man, who has become the benefactor of nature:

> If "to wilful man the injuries that they themselves procure, must be their schoolmasters"—and all beliefs are wilful—then by the same token the propitious evolutions of meaning, which wilful men secure to an *expectant* universe, must be their compensation and their justification. In a *doubtful* and *needy* universe elements must be beggarly, and the development of personal beliefs into experimentally executed systems of actions, is the organized bureau of *philanthropy which confers upon a travailing universe the meaning for which it cries out.*[12] [Italics mine]

Here, instead of "knowing" and leading in development so that "Things come when they are wanted and as they are wanted," the universe is expectant, doubtful, needy, and travailing. Indeed, it "cries out" for "the meaning" which is "conferred upon" it by man's "development of personal beliefs into experimentally executed systems of actions." The Dewey who was to lean heavily on the Romantic poets to exalt man in *Art and Experience* is already quoting from a Romantic poem to reinforce his idea of man as "the thinker, the inquirer, the knower," and benefactor of nature:

> O Dreamer! O Desirer, goer down
> Unto untraveled seas in untried ships,
> O crusher of the unimagined grape,
> On unconceived lips.[13]

IV *Dewey and Darwin*

Whether the greater influence in evolution be assigned to man or to nature, Dewey's reflections on the motive power of this process are considerably different from Darwin's, although we would never discover this from reading Dewey's essay entitled "The Influence of Darwinism on Philosophy"[14] in *The Influence of Darwin on Philosophy*. In this essay Dewey credits Darwin with liberating the mind from the stultifying belief in "some inclusive first cause and some exhaustive final goal,"[15] so that henceforth philosophy could "forswear inquiry after absolute origins and absolute finalities in order to explore specific conditions that generate them."[16]

But Dewey does not seem to understand that Darwin did not dispose so forthrightly of the argument for an "inclusive first cause." At the end of *The Origin of Species*, Darwin—after listing the various characteristics of evolution in summary—definitely attributes the beginning of the process to a "Creator," who had "originally breathed life, with its several powers, into a few forms or into one";[17] and, in *The Descent of Man*, he refers to "the ennobling belief in the existence of an Omnipotent God."[18] The struggle in Darwin's own mind over the problem of the existence of God, which is clearly revealed in the following passage from his *Autobiography* (1876), gives additional evidence of Dewey's misinterpretation of Darwin's attitude:

> Another source of conviction in the existence of God, connected with the reason, and not with the feelings . . . follows from the extreme difficulty or rather impossibility of conceiving this immense and wonderful universe, including man with his capacity of looking far backwards and far into futurity, as the result of blind chance or necessity. When thus reflecting I feel compelled to look to a First Cause having an intel-

ligent mind in some degree analogous to that of man; and I deserve to be called a Theist. This conclusion was strong in my mind about the time, as far as I can remember, when I wrote the "Origin of Species"; and it is since that time that it has very gradually, with many fluctuations, become weaker. But then arises the doubt, can the mind of man, which has, as I fully believe, been developed from a mind as low as that possessed by the lowest animals, be trusted when it draws such grand conclusions?

I cannot pretend to throw the least light on such abstruse problems. The mystery of the beginning of all things is insoluble to us; and I for one must be content to remain an Agnostic.[19]

Darwin, then, did not consider his loss of belief in God as either intellectual or spiritual emancipation. Dewey, already the militant naturalist, deplored belief in an "inclusive first cause" of any kind, although he later decided (against the objections of some of his naturalist followers, especially Sidney Hook) to retain the term *God* but to limit it to the imaginative projection of man's own ideals.

V *Nature as the Ultimate Origin for Life*

Dewey's argument that belief in a transcendent God results in quiescent contemplation instead of fruitful action is perhaps his most frequently repeated negative argument throughout his long career, and it was one which, by its very nature, he could never verify. Indeed, Dewey never indicated whether (or how) he attempted to verify his argument. The majority of beliefs about God certainly does not show that such faith inhibits fruitful action; indeed, most of the great scientists have believed in some form of a transcendent God; others, like Einstein, have believed in an immanent God like that of Spinoza. Dewey condemned this latter type of belief quite as much as he did the former; indeed, any belief that posited the Ideal, whether immanent or transcendent—as in any way already existent—drew his scorn.

Even in this early period, although Dewey usually considers man as equal to, even at times the "benefactor of," nature, there are some evidences that nature has become a kind of immanent substitute for the transcendence in Christianity and Hegelianism that he had abandoned. Because man is the highest expression of nature, he is a collaborator with her in her experiments toward self-improvement (evolution); nevertheless, since man (and all life) originated in nature, she is, to pursue the feminine metaphor, his "mother." Since nature and man are still trying to improve through experimentation, Dewey does not contradict his position denying an already existent Ideal toward which man and nature are trying to conform; but Dewey, in spite of his denial of any concern with ultimate origins, is already very much concerned, as we shall see, with establishing nature as the ultimate origin of all life. In an interview with Max Eastman in 1941 (cf. above, Chapter 1, pp. 13-14) Dewey admitted that his religion, ever since a mystical experience in 1879, had been one of "poetic pantheism" somewhat like that of Wordworth and Whitman. In *Experience and Nature*, as we shall see, he advocates "fidelity to the nature to which we belong," and strongly approves of Justice Holmes's assurance that, if we humbly consider ourselves as "a ganglion within [the universe], we have the infinite behind us."[20] Thus Dewey has some theistic (if pantheistic) presuppositions which must qualify his claims to be an objectively scientific observer of natural processes.

Dewey's view about the collaborative effort of man and nature is in some respects similar to the various forms of emergent evolution—those of philosophers such as Henri Bergson, Hartley B. Alexander, and Alfred North Whitehead. He did not, however, like them, believe in a vitalistic or biocentric conception of the cosmic process as a whole, as he indicated in his essay "The Subject Matter of Metaphysical Inquiry" (1915),[21] which is a development of his decision in the essay on Darwin that what Darwin considered an insoluble question was not really important since "the sole verifiable or fruitful object of knowledge is the particular set of changes that generate the object of study together with the consequences that then flow from it...."[22] Dewey's position in "The Subject Matter of Metaphysical Inquiry" is similar to that which he took later in *Experience and Nature*—a naturalistic metaphysics which "settles upon the more ultimate traits of the world as defining its subject matter, but which frees these traits from confusion with ultimate origins and ultimate ends—that is, from questions of creations and eschatology."[23] But Dewey is by implication hypothesizing about ultimate origins in the following statement:

If everything which is, is a changing thing, the evolution of life and mind indicates the nature of the changes of physico-chemical things and therefore something about those things. It indicates that as purely physical, they are still limited in their interactions; and that as they are brought into more and more complex interactions they exhibit capacities not to be found in an exclusively mechanical world. . . . Without a doctrine of evolution we might be able to say, not that matter *caused* life, but that matter under certain conditions of highly complicated and intensified interactions is living. With the doctrine of evolution, we can add to this statement that the interactions and changes of matter are *themselves* [italics mine] of a kind to bring about that complex and intensified interaction which is life.[24]

The word *themselves*, as well as the tone of the whole passage, indicates that, in Dewey's opinion, no transcendent force beyond nature, operating either during or at any time before these interactions, is needed "to bring about that complex and intensified interaction which is life"; therefore, the ultimate origin is nature itself. Thus, although he proposes that his view will save men "from the futility of concern with ultimate origins,"[25] he is really asserting at great length his own presuppositions about an ultimate nature to which, with great "natural piety," he was to do proper homage in *Experience and Nature*. For, in the course of evolution, as he says, "The striving of man for objects of imagination is a continuation of natural processes; it is something man has learned from the world in which he occurs, not something which he arbitrarily injects into that world. When he adds perception and ideas to these endeavors, it is not after all he who adds; the addition is again the doing of nature and a further complication of its own domain."[26]

In the four essays which Dewey contributed to *Studies in Logical Theory* in 1903,[27] the argument is complicated, both Bernstein and White[28] think, by the presence of more idealist organicism than he was to exhibit in his later work. However, there seems to be convincing evidence that Dewey's resemblance to Hegel was no greater here than in his later work. Dewey makes the following statement about the similarity of his view to one often, though he thinks mistakenly, considered neo-Hegelian. His view and this one, says Dewey, "are at one in denial of the factuality and the possibility of developing fruitful reflection out of antecedent bare existence or mere events. They unite in denying that there is or can be any such thing as mere existence—phenomenon unqualified as respects meaning, whether such phenomenon be psychic or cosmic. They agree that reflective thought grows organically out of an experience which is already organized, and that it functions within such an organism."[29]

White, who quotes this statesment, adds: "Here, of course, we find Dewey reflecting the organicism of his idealist days."[30] But this organicism is not that of his idealist days; it is, as in the essay on "The Reflex Arc Concept in Psychology,"[31] an organicism which has been changed from the Hegelian of the cosmic to the naturalistic type that characterizes Dewey's later writing. That Dewey even in this passage has already made the transition from absolute idealism to naturalistic organicism, or monism, is indicated when he explains what he means in his reference to the three "fundamental distinctions, or divisions of labor, within the reflective process." These are, "first, the *antecedents* or conditions that evoke thought; second, the *datum* or *immediate material* presented to thought; and, third, the *proper content* of thought." "It goes without saying," he adds, "that these are to be discriminated as states of a life-process in the natural history of experience, not as *ready-made* or *ontological* [italics mine].[32]

The mistake of Rudolf Lotze, says Dewey, had been to interpret certain notions, among them the conditions that evoke thought, "as absolute instead of as periodic and methodological."[33] We can assume that Dewey's reje tion of any of these aspects of thought as "ready-made or ontological" indicates that he has abandoned the organicism of his idealist days in favor of one which is part of "the natural history of experience," and that, when he says "that reflective thought grows organically out of experience which is already organized," the "already organized" means no more than "organized by trial and error in the course of evolution" (hence not cosmically, as in Hegel's view, "ready-made or ontological").

If this interpretation is correct, then Dewey is (contrary to White and Bernstein's interpretation of his position), even at this early stage, as far away from Hegel as he was ever to get. He, of course, admitted "that acquaintance with Hegel has left a permanent deposit in my thinking,"[34] and it is easy to point out "holistic" passages here and there in all of his writings; but by 1903 he had already arrived at essentially the same position that he elaborated the rest of his long life. It is true that the post-Hegelian Dewey "seemed," as he said of himself, "to be unstable, chameleon-like, yielding one after another to many diverse and even incompatible influences";[35] but, to repeat, his shifting was limited mainly to the varying degrees of emphasis that he placed from time to time on man and nature. The collaboration between the two was always, after the appearance of man, close enough to be expressed as man-and-nature. But, in this collaboration, sometimes man seems to be more important and at other times nature. During the periods of the nature emphasis, Dewey's "natural piety" and devotion to "mother Nature" become so great that Jacques Maritain has, with some reason, referred to Nature as a kind of Absolute for Dewey, replacing the Christian and Hegelian God of his early period.[36]

VI *The Scientific Method in Education*

Since Dewey's *How We Think*[37] was a preliminary sketch for *Logic: The Theory of Inquiry*,[38] which is examined in detail later, the final book which requires consideration here is *Democracy and Education*, Dewey's most important book in this field and a kind of classic in modern educational theory. Another reason we need to know more about Dewey's views on democracy and education is that they are at the center of his whole philosophy after he abandoned Christianity and Hegelianism—not only in this early period but for the rest of his long life. In his opinion, the vital connection of democracy with scientific experimentation applied (even "deified") as a universal principle is indicated in the following passage. first delivered as an address in 1899 and reprinted in 1910 in *The Influence of Darwin on Philosophy:*

> Democracy is possible only because of a change in intellectual conditions. It implies tools for getting at truth in detail, and day by day, as we go along. Only such possession justifies the surrender of fixed, all-embracing principles to which, as universals, all particulars and individuals are subject for valuation and regulation. . . . Modern life involves the deification of the here and the now; of the specific, the particular, the unique, that which happens once and has no measure of value save such as it brings with itself. Such deification is monstrous fetishism, unless the deity be there; unless the universal lives, moves, and has its being in experience as individualized. This conviction of the value of the individual finds its further expression in psychology.[39]

If this passage seems almost to suggest anarchist individualism, Dewey restores the balance in *Democracy and Education* (first published in 1916) by stating that democracy "is more than a form of government; it is primarily a mode of associated living, of conjoint communicated experience."[40] This associated living and learning are to be made available to all: "A society which makes provision for participation in its good of all its members on equal terms and which secures flexible readjustment of its institutions through interaction of the different forms of associated life is in so far democratic."

As we have said, the philosophy expressed in *Democracy and Education* is basically very little different from Dewey's later one. In the chapter entitled "Education as Growth," for example, children, with proper democratic guidance of their teachers, are to learn "initiative, inventiveness and readaptability—qualities which depend upon the broad and consecutive interaction of specific activities with one another."[41] The students, like intelligent adults, must learn how to apply to all phases of life the scientific method of doubt-inquiry-resolution. Resolution then becomes the incentive for a repetition of the same series on a higher plane—the "continuum of growth," which must not be limited by the idea that the ideal already exists in some absolute or transcendent Being.

The final two chapters—"Theories of Knowledge" and Theories of Morals"—might have been taken from any of Dewey's books written after the turn of the nineteenth century. We have, for example, the following: "The experimental method is new as a scientific resource—as a systematized means of making knowledge, though as old as life as a practical device. . . . For the most part, its significance is regarded as belonging to certain technical and merely physical matters. It will doubtless take a long time to secure the perception that it holds equally as to the forming and testing of ideas in social and moral matters. Men still want the crutch of dogma, of beliefs fixed by authority. . . ."[42]

It we think that the experimental method in moral matters might have real dangers for immature adults and certainly for children during the educational process, Dewey reassures us by telling us (in the chapter entitled "Experience and Thinking") exactly how the danger can be avoided, presumably by men or (with some democratic, adult guidance) children:

Thinking is the accurate and deliberate instituting of connections between what is done and its consequences. . . . The projection of consequences means a proposed or tentative solution. To perfect this hypothesis, existing conditions have to be carefully scrutinized and the implications of the hypothesis developed—an operation called reasoning. Then the suggested solution—the idea or theory—has to be tested by acting upon it. If it brings about certain consequences, certain determinate changes, in the world, it is accepted as valid. Otherwise it is modified, and another trial made.[43]

Of course, as will be said elsewhere in this book, such a procedure is a standard one for scientific discoveries, invention, and so on, and should be taught to the child; but a higher criterion for morals than a prudential consideration of consequences is needed. Even on the level of prudence, the following criticism by Sister Joseph Mary Raby will express the deep conviction of the great majority of us who have had experience in secondary-school teaching in either private or public schools: "In a Dewey school, the leading principle of the tentativeness of all truths, moral included, would meet with difficulty in practice for two reasons. In the first place, the immaturity of a child, organism, or person, would limit the application of such a principle in practice; the implications would be almost impossible for a child to comprehend. Second, if this principle were really to be exemplified in ways adapted to children's abilities, the result would be, I think, personal disorganization. We are all weary of the word 'security,' but children need what this word stands for."[44]

In *Democracy and Education* Dewey makes many helpful suggestions for developing the child's interest by meaningful activities instead of merely routine drill. From these suggestions grew the widely influential movement called "progressive education," which flourished in America during the 1920's and 1930's until its excesses resulted in its decline. The famous concluding passage of Dewey's *Democracy and Education* describes the purpose and nature of such a school:

> The two theories chiefly associated with the separation of learning from activity, and hence from morals, are those which cut off inner disposition and motive—the conscious personal factor—and deeds as purely physical and outer; and which set action from interest in opposition to that from principle. Both of these separations are overcome in an educational scheme where learning is the accompaniment of continuous activities or occupations which have a social aim and utilize the materials of typical social situations. For under such conditions the school becomes itself a form of social life, a miniature community and one in close interaction with other modes of associated experience beyond school walls.[45]

Such was the very persuasive plan outlined by Dewey, and some schools with imaginative teachers and bright pupils were able to improve the motivation of learning by following Dewey's ideas insofar as they were practicable. But the limitations of their practicality have again been well expressed by Sister Joseph Mary Raby: "In the 'integrated curriculum,' the usual school subjects were to grow out of the activities of the project. The mastery of subjects was often less than mastery. To learn the arithmetic, the spelling, the reading, as need arises in the pursuit of a project is an unrealistic undertaking. It would require angelic intelligence to see steadily and whole all the relations involved and the foundations for them. The human mind, and certainly a child's mind, had to proceed less totally, and step by step."[46]

Indeed, in his book *Experience and Education*, Dewey himself makes some extensive, adverse criticism of the progressive schools. He refers to "the absence of the adequate intellectual and moral organization in the newer type of school."[47] And he says it is an "unfortunate idea that progressive schools can to a very large extent ignore the past."[48] If this reference to the past and to moral organization seems like a change in Dewey's idea of unlimited experimentation, it is not really so. Dewey thinks that the defects are due to insufficient and ineffective experimentation—a failure, in other words, to evaluate the experiments by observing their consequences so that "an experiential continuum" might be maintained. Never for a moment after his early abandonment of all forms of transcendence did this devoted follower of the scientific method doubt its universal efficacy. If scientific method failed to produce desirable consequences, all that was needed, in his earnest opinion, was more scientific method.

The above criticism of Dewey is by no means intended to imply that he was wrong in wishing to use the school to promote democratic cooperation that destroys class distinctions. He recognizes the difficulty of such an achievement in our present society, even in our supposedly classless America. "The school," he says, "cannot immediately escape from the ideals set by prior social conditions. But it should contribute through the type of intellectual and emotional disposition which it forms to the improvement of those conditions. . . . To organize education so that natural active tendencies shall be fully enlisted in doing something, while seeing to it that the doing requires observation, the acquisition of information, and the use of a constructive imagination, is what most needs to be done to improve social conditions."[49]

VII *Democrat and Religious Prophet*

Dewey was a great democrat; and, as Father John Blewett has indicated, he at one time considered Christianity, rightly interpreted, to be most compatible with democracy. However, as Father Blewett says, "quite early in his career [in the late 1880's] Dewey denied God a ticket of admission to the democratic world then allegedly forming and wrote off Christianity as irremediably perverse."[50] Father Blewett calls Dewey a prophet of a religion of democracy, the "Celestial Ethic"; but it seems to us more appropriate to consider him more broadly as the prophet of a religion of science and nature, which would include democracy as a way of life. Expressed in a slightly different way, Dewey's religion may be said to have been one whose high priest was a democratic, and yet heroic, man; whose creed was the scientific method to be applied, eventually, in democratic man's good time, to all aspects of man's life; and whose prophet, the voice crying in the wilderness, was John Dewey. We hear the words of the prophet in the closing passage of "From Absolutism to Experimentalism":

> Seen in the long perspective of the future, the whole of European history is a provincial episode. I do not expect to see in my day a genuine, as distinct from a forced and artificial, integration of thought. But a mind that is not too egoistically impatient can have faith that that his unification will issue in its season. Meantime a chief task of those who call themselves philosophers is to help get rid of the useless lumber that blocks our highways of thought, and strive to make straight and open the paths that lead to the future. Forty years spent in wandering in a wilderness like that of the present is not a sad fate—unless one attempts to make himself believe that the wilderness is after all itself the promised land.[51]

CHAPTER 3

Experimental Naturalism with Religious Overtones
Dewey's *Experience and Nature*

WE can agree with Professor Bernstein that Dewey's most important books appeared in the final period that began with *Experience and Nature* in 1925 (second edition, 1929). This book alone could have made the reputation of Dewey as an important philosopher. It is a difficult book because its multifarious ideas—on experience, nature, logic, metaphysics, esthetics, ethics, and religion—are closely packed in complex, often awkwardly constructed sentences, which are characteristic of Dewey's style (except in the more popular works like *A Common Faith*). As for organization, allowances must be made, of course, for the fact that these abstract topics are bound to overlap and that Dewey is trying to cover the whole range of his philosophy in one work. An impressive work, it is probably Dewey's most important single colume. A short summary may be helpful.

Experience, properly understood, is the best way to understand nature. Experience does not divide "subject and object, but contains them both in an unanalyzed totality." This totality includes not only cognitive objects but noncognitive emotional qualities, the second as well as the first being objective in nature. Instead of positing a purely theoretical security and certainty, experience recognizes that existence fortunately contains both the precarious and the stable, for we would without the precarious become morally and intellectually soft. The way of wisdom is to understand that nature consists of events rather than substances and that these events, through the scientific method, can be controlled (planned) so that they constitute a progressive change from beginnings to ends which mean consummation and fulfillment. When such ends are reached through natural means, there is a tendency to repeat and perpetuate them; and such a tendency is the foundation for value.

The scientific method, or knowledge just referred to, consists of social participation and communication made effective by language and other tools. Indeed, mind is not only a function of social interactions in their most complex form but is also a genuine character of natural events instead of something miraculously introduced from above. Mind also has an individual aspect and may be identified with selfhood. Mind, from this standpoint, uses the variable, or the unstable, qualities of natural events constructively as the starting points of new observations, hypotheses, and experiments.

A consideration of life as the link between physical nature and experience solves the mind-body problem. At the pre-mental level, natural organisms have feelings which are natural events and which distinguish them from inanimate things. When these natural events become more complex through the developement of lanuage and other tools so that there is communication and objects are shared in common and universalized, then these events have taken on mental properties. The meanings that form mind become consciousness or ideas when meanings which are not clear are reconstructed. Such reconstruction is the basis for an alert and effective mind.

The highest development of both experience and nature may be found in art, in which natural materials are reshaped for pure enjoyment of mind.

I *Experience as Disclosure of Nature*

So that the concept of experience may furnish the basis for Dewey's empirical method, he makes in the beginning his definition of experience a very broad one. He agrees with William James that experience is a "double-barreled" word "in that it recognizes in its primary integrity no division between act and material, subject and object, but contains them both in an unanalyzed totality."[1] Experience "is *of* as well as *in* nature,"[2] and the connection is made even closer when he says that experience is not only the "method for dealing with nature" but also "the goal in which nature is disclosed for what it is." The method to which he refers for dealing with nature is his version of the empirical method (the method of experience) which recognizes that the "unanalyzed totality" includes not only cognitive objects (objects which can be known) but does not favor them and their characteristics "at the expense of traits that excite desire, command action and produce passion. . . . "[3] Dewey insists that these noncognitive emotional (or what Santayana called "tertiary") qualities are objective in nature instead of being merely subjective traits of the experiencing subject. This interpretation, one by no means universally accepted by Dewey's fellow naturalists, is discussed later.

More important to notice here is the harshly polemical tone (never long absent from Dewey's later writing) of his attack on the idea of a transcendent Being or God. The way to discover the nature of the good is to experiment through Dewey's version of the empirical method; traits which may be considered good should never be "transformed . . . into fixed traits of real Being."[4] Dewey, as we have noted, was later to consider the word *God* as acceptable if it meant no more than the ideals which man generates out of his own experience. This exaltation of man was at times to be modified by giving much of the credit to nature, which "realizes its own potentialities in intelligence," along with various statements to the effect that such addition of perception and ideas to natural processes was not due to man but was "the doing of nature and a further complication of its own domain."[5]

But always, as here, Dewey insisted that belief in a transcendent Being "ignores the need of action to effect the better"[6] and rests in mere contemplation. So convinced was he of the truth of this belief that, in his rewriting of the first chapter of *Experience and Nature* in the second edition, he added the following statement not found in the first edition: "The transcendental philosopher [he is referring not to a Transcendentalist like Emerson but to a believer in a transcendent God] has probably done more than the professed sensualist and materialist to obscure the potentialities of daily experience for joy and for self-regulation."[7] The extravagance of this statement is too obvious to require comment, but the opinion expressed is not untypical and, in connection with other more restrained statements of this point of view, is considered later.

II *Union of Hazardous and Stable*

Although Professor Randall tells us that it is "not difficult to exhibit Dewey as an Aristotelian more Aristotelian than Aristotle himself,"[8] Dewey finds Aristotle sadly deficient in the central emphasis of his philosophy: "His [Aristotle's] whole theory of forms

and ends is a theory of the superiority in Being of rounded-out fixities. His physics is a fixation of ranks or grades of necessity and
contingency so sorted that necessity measures dignity and equals
degree of reality, while contingency and change measure degrees
of deficiency of Being. The empirical impact and sting of the mixture of universality and singularity and chance is evaded by parcell-
ing out the regions of space so that they have their natural abode
in different portions of nature."[9] Kant's hypothesis of a noumenal
realm of reason makes him also, in Dewey's opinion, guilty "of a
conversion of a moral insight to be made good in action into an
antecedent metaphysics of existence or a general theory of knowledge."[10]

The objection that Dewey has to all "classic, orthodox [Platonic
and Christian along with Aristotelian, Kantian, and other] philosophies" that posit the existence of an ideal realm is that their
goal is possession of this realm through contemplation and, as a
result, "effort is rendered useless. . . ."[11] It would be interesting
to have had Kant's answer to such a criticism because of his early
revolt against the pietistic substitution of ritual for dutiful action
and his perpetual emphasis upon the necessity of man's doing his
duty, which alone, he said, made man worthy of being considered
the highest object in creation.[12]

We might think that Dewey would be attracted to philosophies
of change, becoming, process, or flux; but he finds that all of them,
from Heraclitus to Bergson, "also indicate the intensity of the crav-
ing for the sure and fixed. They have deified change by making it
universal, regular, sure."[13] If such an attack on the idea of change
sounds a little strange, from one who in *The Reconstruction of Philosophy* hammers at the necessity of change—even saying in several
places that change should be introduced artificially—the only explanation seems to be Dewey's warning that in his post-Hegelian
days he might "seem to be unstable, chamelon-like, yielding one
after another to many diverse and even incompatible influences."[14]

Even in *Experience and Nature* Dewey wants change, as we have
seen, from all the great philosophies of the past and present that
posit an ideal realm to his own system which, he says, does not
"deify" but strongly emphasizes progressive change or evolution
on a purely experimental basis. His swift, sweeping, and perhaps
not too objective summary of these philosophies stresses only one
point: they all exalt contemplation of the imagined good at the

expense of the attainment of the real good. "The most widespread of these classificatory devices, the one of greatest appeal, is that which divides existence into the supernatural and the natural."[15] Even the more subtle philosophers who accept the metaphysical are condemned since their "most cherished metaphysical distinctions seem to be but learned counterparts . . . for these rough crude notions of supernatural and natural, divine and human, in popular belief."[16] Dewey is the great philosopher of the experimental approach to knowledge or truth, but here, somewhat dogmatically and vaguely, he asserts "the *fact* [italics mine] that it is the intricate mixture of the stable and the precarious, the fixed and the unpredictably novel, the assured and the uncertain, in existence which sets mankind upon that love of wisdom which forms philosophy."[17]

The meaning of this somewhat puzzling "fact" will appear a little later, but first we must note his disappointment in finding it "denied" by "that striking division into a superior true realm of being and lower, illusory, insignificant or phenomenal realm which characterizes metaphysical systems as unlike as those of Plato and Democritus, St. Thomas and Spinoza, Aristotle and Kant, Descartes and Comte, Haeckel and Mrs. Eddy";[18] to this group of misguided dualists Dewey adds for good measure Bertrand Russell and Santayana. Earlier, in *Ethics*,[19] he had praised the Judaeo-Christian religion as a moral one which emphasized the going of good rather than the mere contemplation of it; but, in his concentration here on the uses of science, he lumps together all belief in the supernatural as being reactionary and ineffectively "contemplative," and all idealistic philosophies as being inadequate because their basic idea is that psychic existence is "sure to be inherently more ideal than the physical."

Dewey, in other words, allows nothing, not even Bertrand Russell's theory of mathematical structures as "the region of absolute necessity,"[20] to take us away from "the union of the hazardous and the stable, of the incomplete and the recurrent," which "is the condition of all experienced satisfaction as truly as of our predicaments and problems. While it is the source of ignorance, error and failure of expectation, it is the source of the delight which fulfillments bring."[21] As if this sentence seems a little foggy, Dewey shows in the next one that he intends the "ignorance, error and failure of expectation" to be part of the preparatory difficulty which makes the eventual fulfillment, the "stable," more satisfactory than it would have been without the "deviations and resistances." This intent would have been clear in the beginning if Dewey had referred to the triumph of the "stable" over the "hazardous" instead of to their "union." His preference for trying to make opposites unite is, of course, a residue from his Hegelian days.

Indeed, such "holistic" passages may be found frequently throughout his works, as Dewey himself recognized when he said, in his autobiographical essay "From Absolutism to Experimentalism,"[22] that his knowledge of Hegel was a lasting influence. He still sounds Hegelian when he says that the traditional concept of the unstable as existing only to prepare for the stable should be inverted to state that the stable exists only for the transition to the unstable,[23] the unstable of course being considered as part of the dynamic movement onward to something better. A little later, however,[24] he finds the evanescence of the good a source of sober (if not somber) reflection; and he speaks of himself as reporting not what is desirable but what is factual.

The characteristic of asserting as fact what is only his *ex cathedra* opinion becomes rather annoying at times in Dewey, and he becomes far less assured when answering some of his more skillful critics, especially Reichenbach, in the Schilpp volume. Dewey, for example, considers that affective (emotional) qualities are products of the doings of nature. A satisfaction (fulfilling desire) or nonsatisfaction (frustrating desire) is an objective thing with objective conditions (in other words, as objectively valid a part of our nature as intellect); and "the favoring of cognitive objects . . . at the expense of traits that excite desire . . . is an example of partiality and partisanship in philosophy."[25] When Reichenbach objects that satisfaction, or any other affective quality, is not intersubjective (and not a scientifically valid object of valuation) but very demonstrably varies with the nature of the observer,[26] Dewey gives the following rather vague answer, which seems a little like hedging:

Correlations between changes that form *conditions* of desires, etc., and changes that form their *consequences* when acted upon, have the same standing and function in this field that physical objects have in their field.

There are many *practical* difficulties to be overcome in developing the methods of inquiry that will enable conclusions regarding such correlations to be reached. But as distinct from the position taken by

Mr. Reichenbach there is no inherent theoretical bar on my view to some day succeeding.[27]

This prophecy seems about as imprecisely stated as the final sentence is awkward; but, if we omit the prophecy and recall what Dewey has said elsewhere, his more plausible defense for making affective qualities objectively a part of nature would read something like this: Man is part of nature. When man adds perception and ideas to natural processes, "it is not after all he who adds; the addition is again the doing of nature and a further complication of its own domain."[28] The same would be true for desire, love, and all the other affective qualities; and Dewey even adds human reverie and fantasy to his list of objective features of nature.

When Reichenbach and others object to this argument by pointing out how these affective qualities vary from individual to individual and are thus bound to be subjective, Dewey answers that he did not consider these qualities objective in the sense of being the only basis of ethical norms. From one standpoint, the difference is merely a matter of terminology; but there is, nonetheless, a basic difference because Dewey wants to make morals and esthetics as objective as the physical and natural sciences—and as amenable to the scientific method—while Reichenbach says that "the theory of values needs no artificial spine of a quasi-cognitive theory of values."[29] Between Reichenbach's admittedly subjective theory of values and Dewey's, which is "objective" in that he makes man's "tertiary" qualities (desire, affection, etc.) an objective part of nature, there does not seem to be much to choose; but Dewey, from this angle, seems to have held his own with reasonable effectiveness against a dissenting fellow naturalist.

The empirical process of reaching a satisfactory solution, Dewey explains, will involve reflective thinking, genuinely scientific inquiry, experimentation: "At no point or place is there any jump outside empirical, natural objects and their relations. Thought and reason . . . . consist of the procedures intentionally employed in the application to each other of the unsatisfactorily confused and indeterminate on one side and the regular and stable on the other."[30] Dewey does not want us to think that he has forgotten mother Nature, so he balances the account by reminding us of another "fact": "The situation [nature or the universe] is not indifferent to man, because it forms man as a desiring, striving, thinking, feeling creature."[31] Does this dogmatic statement mean that man gets some help from nature? In one way Dewey would say yes, because man is part of nature; this is really nature operating at a highly complex level. "Choice," he says, "is not arbitrary, not in a universe like this one, a world which is not finished and which has not consistently made up its mind where it is going and what it is going to do."[32] Here again, in the interest of "natural piety," Dewey is giving the credit to nature; for, as he says later,[33] "in the entire human predicament, this human situation falls wholly within nature." When man adds perception and ideas to natural processes, "it is not after all he who adds; the addition is again the doing of nature and a further complication of its own domain."[34]

III *Natural Teleology*

Dewey also stresses the human importance (neglected, he says, by most philosophers) of the "direct phase of experience, in which objects are not a matter of sensations, ideas, beliefs or knowledge, but are something had and enjoyed."[35] "The history of man shows that man takes his enjoyment neat, and at as short range as possible."[36] All this man does with Dewey's approval; and, if we think that he is becoming moderately Dionysian, we are correct—but we are not to think that he is not at the same time strongly Apollonian: "Immediate enjoyment and suffering are the conclusive exhibition and evidence that nature has its finalities as well as its relationships."[37]

The "relationships," which are here apparently designed to be the Apollonian part of Dewey's synthesis, do not prevent the suggestion of incipient pathos in his emphasis on the "evanescence" of "whatever is immediately consummatory and precious." We would have expected Dewey to find enduring satisfaction in his reversal of the traditional emphasis on "the general, recurrent and extensive" as "the worthy and superior kind of Being," since he tells us that "the universal and stable are *important* [italics mine] because they are the instrumentalities, the efficacious conditions, of the occurrence of the unique, unstable and passing."[38] He asserts such a reversal of the traditional hierarchy of greater and less reality to be a fact, but hastens to add that "A reporter is not necessarily to blame for the state of things that he reports."[39]

The just noted, rather somber, mood (rather infrequent with Dewey) is only temporary and is another example of the "unstable, chameleon-like"[40] quality which applies to both his moods and his ideas; but one idea always remains constant—his exaltation of democracy. He expresses it in *Experience and Nature* by his attack on the perverted Greek idea of democracy. Among the ancient Greeks, he says, "The conception that thought is the final and complete end of nature became a 'rationalization' of an existing division of classes in society," the leisure class being the "thinkers" and the working class the less important "doers."[41] However, Dewey gives the Greeks credit for making some improvement: as time went on, he says, "The gods recede into twilight . . . . Worship becomes moral. Medicine, war, and the crafts desert the temple and the altar of the patron-god of the guild, as inventions, tools, techniques of action and works multiply."[42] But this period "of confident expansion," he says, "did not endure"[43]; and it was soon succeeded by a return to the supernatural.

In spite of Dewey's modified attack on the Greeks, it should be noticed that his views on "natural teleology" owe much to them. For example, the following sentence, in which he describes Aristotle's concept of forms, is not unlike Dewey's idea about the development of mind: "The actualization in an organic body of the forms that are found in things constitutes mind as the end of nature."[44] As Dewey sees it, the trouble with this concept is that its emphasis was contemplative rather than social and dynamic: "An immediate contemplative possession and enjoyment of objects, dialectically ordered, was interpreted as defining both true knowledge and the highest end and good of nature."[45] Dewey emphasizes the idea that ends are only transitions to higher ends rather than "closures of change,"[46] but he insists again, like the Greeks, that these ends are not "entertained in individual minds independent of nature"[47] (as the scientific revolution of the seventeenth century mistakenly maintained), but are evidences of a "natural teleology,"[48] which, however, admits nothing "transcendental . . . outside of events, whether called God or Will or the Unknowable."[49] It should be remembered, however (and this fact Dewey does not mention), that, for most of the great thinkers in ancient Greece, natural teleology did not exclude a Being or Force superior to and directing nature.

Not even modern science, strangely enough, escapes Dewey's severe strictures. He praises it because it "represents a generalized recognition and adoption of the point of view of the useful arts, for it proceeds by employment of a similar operative technique of manipulation and reduction."[50] But modern science became involved in a metaphysical problem when it retained from Classical philosophy the notion of knowledge as immediate possession of Being: "If the proper object of science is a mathematico-mechanical world (as the achievements of science have proved to be the case) and if the object of science defines the true and perfect reality (as the perpetuation of the classic tradition asserted), then how can the objects of love, appreciation—whether sensory or ideal—and devotion be included within true reality?"[51]

Dewey's answer to this problem is extensive but essentially simple. Knowledge is not possession or grasp but a satisfactory, though never permanent, solution of a problematic situation: "the proper objects of science are nature in its instrumental characters."[52] We don't have the mind-versus-body, or the matter-versus-spirit, problem because these qualities, which we artificially divide into realms, are really simply functional characteristics of nature conducting at a high, complex level the operations which we call "knowledge" and which are to be judged by their consequences. Under this all-inclusive system, both the individual and the combination of individuals into unified wholes receive their proportional emphases without individualistic anarchy or the subjection of the individual to laws of uniformity. Morals also become effectively a part of nature without the (to Dewey unbearable) "supposition of another kind of Being from that with which natural sciences are concerned." In short, all problems—physical, mental, moral, or spiritual—are to be approached experimentally through the method of the modern non-metaphysical scientific method, in the practice of which "knowledge is an affair of *making* sure, not of grasping antecedently given sureties."[53]

When Dewey temporarily stops his attack on the Transcendent and its supposedly "antecedently given sureties," we can agree with most of what he says about "Nature, Communication and Meaning." It is undoubtedly true that exponents of philosophic idealism have frequently overemphasized the separation of meaning and essences from meaning communicated between human beings and shared by them in fruitful interaction. Dewey's practical emphasis here is needed, and he maintains a balance that has been lost by some of the philosophers who concentrate on language. Dewey, for example, says that a sound, gesture, or written mark "does not become a word by declaring a mental existence; it becomes a word by gaining meaning; and it gains meaning when its use establishes a general community of action."[54] Discourse, for Dewey, consists of "the forms which things assume under the pressure and opportunity of social cooperation and exchange."[55]

But Dewey is less successful when he relates meaning to essence. Essence he calls "the distilled import of existence . . . identified with those consummatory consequences which the thing has when conditions are felicitous . . . a legitimate, practical measure of reality in terms of importance. . . ."[56] We can agree with Dewey about the practical value of essence thus defined, but we cannot agree with him that this is the only kind of essence or that existence precedes every kind of essence—in his sense, for example,[57] of "an existence having meaning and potential essence." His limitation of essence to the practical does not necessarily exclude (though he seems to think that it does) the Transcendent Being in Whom essence and existence are one and Who is the source of this human existence described so enthusiastically by Dewey—the system of the naturalist characterized by what he calls "the modern [why modern?] discovery of inner experience, of a realm of purely personal events that are always at the individual's command, and that are his exclusively as well as inexpensively for refuge, consolation and thrill. . . ."[58]

IV   *The "Old Self" and "New Self"*

In the chapter entitled "Nature, Mind and Subject" in *Experience and Nature*, Dewey deplores the exaggeration of the ego in modern philosophy, although he emphasizes the importance of *"freedom* of thought" so long as this means "freedom of *thinking,"*[59] which is not an escape into the ivory tower " 'inward landscape' . . . seized upon by Romanticism as the exclusive truth of experience,"[60] but which is genuinely constructive experimentation resulting in valuable social consequences. The movement of thought should "terminate, as in the later philosophy of Josiah Royce, with a 'community of selves,' . . . but the intervening insertion of a transcendent ego remains as a plague."[61]

Dewey insists that we can receive help from nature but never from a "transcendent ego" or transcendent Being of whatever kind. The kind of help we get from nature, however, is never quite clear because Dewey always wants to protect himself from attack on both sides of his natural fortress. We may consider the following sentence as an example of the relation of man to nature: "Only when obstacles are treated as challenges to remaking of personal desire and thought, so that the latter integrate with the movement of nature and by participation direct its consequences, are opposition and duality rightly understood."[62] How are the consequences to be directed? To what extent are personal desire and thought to be remade and why? Does "integration with the movement of nature" mean that the obstacle has been overcome or that desire has been "remade" so that the obstacle is accepted without being removed? Or does the "remaking of desire" mean that what was formerly considered to be an obstacle is no longer so considered? In that case, are the "consequences" of nature really "directed" in any other way than by a subjective change of our attitude in the direction if not to the extent of Pollyanna?

The reason that Dewey's ideas have been so variously interpreted by so many different critics is that he has many ambiguous sentences, like the one just considered, which seem to promise various contradictory things. Dewey, without doing so specifically, seems to promise a happy union of all these contradictory traits of existence. Except in a few places where he regrets the evanescence of what is precious (such regret being itself a form of Romanticism), his thought dwells in the essentially Romantic light of a speculative "synthesis," which synthesizes usually by merely stating (without proof) that nature has been mistakenly called "mechanical," although it is really a happy "conjunction . . . of whimsical contingency and lawful uniformity."[63]

In humanity (nature at a complex level), these traits are expressed as "distinctive opacity of bias and preference conjoined with plasticity and permeability of needs and likings."[64] Fortunately, in Dewey's roseate view the "plasticity" can so control the "opacity" that the individual's "activities set out to remake conditions in accord with desire" (with apparently none of Omar Khayyám's disillusionment), and in this gallant effort, "intelligence is born . . . mind as individualized, initiating, adventuring, experimenting, dissolving."[65] This Dewey is the religious one, the prophet of a new religion, in which (without the hindrance of belief in a transcendent Being) "the old self is put off and the new self is only forming, and the form it finally takes will depend upon the unforeseeable result of an adventure."[66] Before Dewey can initiate us into the pragmatic rites of his new cult, however, he must make us "understand operations of the self as the tool of tools, *the* means in all use of means"[67];

and he proposes to do so in the chapter entitled "Nature, Life, and Body-Mind."

V *Continuity from Physical to Mental*

The key word in understanding this "tool of tools" is *continuity*. Dewey's whole concern is to convince us that there is really no mystery about the development from the inanimate to the animate and from the animate to the mental; the process is simply natural. He calls the inanimate *physical* and the animate *psycho-physical*, and the latter is distinguished from the former only by "the possession of certain qualities and efficacies not displayed by the inanimate."[68] "Thus conceived, there is no problem of the relation of physical *and* psychic. There are specifiable empirical events marked by distinctive qualities and efficacies. There is first of all, *organization*. . . . The problem is one of definite factual inquiry."[69]

If we should ask how organization is to be explained, Dewey would simply answer that "Organization is an empirical trait of some events . . . no matter how false are doctrines about it which have . . . construed it as evidence of a special force or entity called life or soul."[70] Dewey's attribution of falseness to a view which he has disproved only by asserting that his own opposing view is true might be construed as a little dogmatic for one who insists on carefully checking all his assertions so that they have at least "warranted assertibility," but we must attend his argument. At least there is organization in the lowest animate forms, a point which nobody would care to deny. Then Dewey explains the appearance of mind; he says that all along the problem is one (and he implies only one) of "definite factual inquiry." But, if that were true, we would not need his elaborately argumentative defense of the naturalistic development of life. The truth is that Dewey is speculating just as much as those who appeal to a transcendent God for a partial explanation of this development. His whole concern, here at least, is to demonstrate that there is not only no need for a belief in anything more than nature but that such a belief is a positive hindrance to the good life.

In pursuing this "definite factual inquiry," Dewey is merely following the explanation that is fairly commonplace in textbooks on biological evolution: "As life is a character of events in a peculiar condition of organization, and 'feeling' is a quality of life-forms marked by complexly mobile and discrimination responses, so 'mind' is an added property assumed by a feeling creature, when it reaches the organized interaction with other living creatures which is language, communication. . . . The distinction between physical, psycho-physical, and mental is thus one of levels of increasing complexity and intimacy of interaction among natural events."[71] Dewey thinks that he has successfully established his view when he asserts that "psycho-physical phenomena and higher mental phenomena may be admitted in their full empirical reality, without recourse to a dualistic breach in historic, existential continuity."[72] (This part of Dewey's argument seems much like Bertrand Russell's argument for a "neutral monism.")[73]

Dewey will not use the word "cause," since such a word implies that what causes is superior ontologically to its effect. If we should ask him why the change from simple to complex, he would again appeal to "empirical reality" and deny that the question was really a question at all—a disposal device frequently used by Mrs. Susanne Langer in her *Philosophy in a New Key* (for Dewey, it would be a "reconstructed" key). Sometimes, perhaps in a less cautious mood, Dewey does give an implied answer to the question of cause, although he again would call it only an "interaction of natural events."

As we have noted, Dewey is always concerned to make everything in the development of life appear perfectly "natural" and therefore not mysterious. He does not completely avoid the term *mystery*, as we see in the following two sentences: "But the wonder and mystery do not seem other than the wonder and mystery that there should be such a thing as nature, as existential events, at all, and that in being they should be what they are. . . . It may be mystery that there should be thinking, but it is no mystery that if there is thinking it should contain in a 'present' phase, affairs remote in space and in time, even to geologic ages, future eclipes and far away stellar systems."[74]

Even here, however, he plays down the mystery by dwelling on the "empirical reality" of mind as composed of "features which emerge when 'body' is engaged in a wider, more complex and interdependent situation."[75] He then says that the emergence of mind is not a mystery at all, not even a "problem to be solved: it is an expression of the common fact that anything changes according to the interacting field it enters."[76] Later he decides that, after all, there may be a problem; but it can readily be solved if we only consider all the connections and the continuity beginning with (of course) Mother Nature: "To see the organism *in* nature, the nervous system in the organism, the brain in the nervous system, the cortex in the brain is the answer to the problems which haunt philosophy."[77]

And Dewey is not referring merely to the speculative problems but also to the moral problems. Failing to see all the connections beginning with Mother Nature and proceeding "in a moving, growing never finished process . . . . we trust most unreservedly in our deliberate beliefs to the isolated and specific . . . to the unconscious and subconscious. . . ."[78] In the next chapters of *Experience and Nature* Dewey proposes to instruct us in the elevation of this narrow preoccupation to the level of consciousness, so that we may clearly see all the connections back through the ages with nature and live at the high moral and esthetic level to which this knowledge will bring us (*how* is never quite clear).

In the chapter entitled "Existence, Ideas and Consciousness" the same theme is continued with further analysis of the characteristics of nature functioning at the human level. Dewey makes some common-sense statements about the proper uses to which the subconscious (by which he seems to mean in this instance *intuition*) may be put in "mathematics, or philosophizing far away from concrete situations, or in a highly cultivated fine art," and he warns appropriately against dependence on the subconscious "in connection with intimate matters of self-regulation in health, morals, social affairs."[79]

Dewey here emphasizes the importance of the past in a way that to some extent compensates for his apparent overemphasis in most places on the necessity of "reconstruction" of that past through experimentation in all phases of life, including morals and religion: "the purport of past affairs," he says,[80] "is present in the momentary cross-sectional idea in a way which is more intimate, direct and pervasive than the way of recall." This statement might well recall T. S. Eliot's presentness of the past, or Whitehead's "emotional continuity of the past with the present" as the "basic element from which springs the self-creation of each temporal occasion,"[81] but Dewey is far from embracing Christianity, as does Eliot. And for Dewey experimentation in the present, rather than the continuity of the past with the present as for Whitehead, is the basic element in creative progress. The distinction is in the emphasis.

The rest of Dewey's chapter is concerned (in an extended, repetitive manner) with the distinction among the types of meaning attached to varying kinds of perception. We need to notice here only his activist theory of knowledge, which cannot "take place without an overt act of taking and employing things on the basis of their meaning. . . ."[82] He answers those critics who have accused him of "ignoring the place and charm of contemplation" by saying: "Contemplation assuredly has a place. But when it is ultimate, and is a fruition, knowing has stepped out of the picture; the vision is esthetic."[83] This subordination of the esthetic might seem to differ from the emphasis which he places on it in his next chapter and then nine years later (1934) in his *Art as Experience*—a problem considered later. Earlier, it will be remembered, Dewey promised to acquaint us with the "operations of the self as the tool of tools, *the* means in all use of means. . .,"[84] but at the end of this promised explanation it is still difficult to see how the knowledge (available in any good textbook on physiological psychology) which he imparts to us about the intricacies of consciousness is going to save those who need saving from the dangers of living by the subconscious.

Dewey repeatedly denounces idealistic theories of knowledge and (rather unfairly) makes them almost synonymous with reverie. He assures us (perhaps unnecessarily) that "the view of complete separation of existential consciousness from connection with phyical things cannot be maintained in view of what is known of its specifiable connections with organic conditions, and of the intimate, unbroken connection of organic with extra-organic events."[85] Again his interpretation of the views of his opponents seems inaccurate, if not an actual travesty: "It is possible to understand the regret with which some persons contemplate the passage of thought into act; to them it seems the obsequies of an idea; thought has been dissipated in an outward mechanical sequence."[86] Belief in a transcendent God, says Dewey, leads to this kind of barren contemplation. The view that releases all man's creative powers is that which says that nature creates its own teleology. "When consciousness is connected with nature, the mystery becomes a luminous revelation of the operative interpenetration in nature of the efficient and the fulfilling."[87]

VI *Art, the Culmination of Nature*

In Chapter IX ("Experience, Nature and Art") Dewey gives a

definition of the esthetic which apparently contradicts his identification in Chapter VIII of the esthetic with the contemplative and hence the inferior. The only real form of knowledge he says in Chapter VIII, is that which occurs when a meaning is acted upon, and such action is not esthetic. But in Chapter IX, as later in *Art as Experience*, art is for Dewey the highest form of activity—"art—the mode of activity that is charged with meanings capable of immediately enjoyed possession—is the complete culmination of nature, and 'science' is properly a handmaiden that conducts natural events to this happy issue."[88] There might seem to be a contradiction also between his earlier assertion that immediate data are not to be considered knowledge, which comes only after we have taken time to note the consequences, and his assertion here that art, "the complete culmination of nature," "is charged with meanings capable of immediately enjoyed possession."[89] Yet Dewey is here, as often, in one of his combining moods in which there is supposedly a synthesis of opposites. The best art, he says, is that which best does what nature does: combines "spontaneity and necessity, the regular and the novel, the finished and the beginning . . . . the instrumental and the consummatory. Any activity that is simultaneously both, rather than in alternation and displacement, is art."[90] Of course, art is also the "culmination of nature"; and, as usual, nature is given the supreme credit.

Dewey's definition of the word *art* is finally extended to include everything of which he highly approves. For example, "Thinking is pre-eminently an art; knowledge and propositions which are the products of thinking, are words of art, as much so as statuary and symphonies."[91] Scientific method is also an art, which "does not set its product, knowledge, apart from other works of art."[92] Again Dewey the preacher deplores the fact that the scientific method has not been applied to human and social affairs as it has to inanimate nature: "When an art of thinking as appropriate to human and social affairs has grown up as that used in dealing with distant stars, it will not be necessary to argue that science is one among the arts and among the works of art. . . . The separation of science from art, and the division of arts into those concerned with mere means and those concerned with ends in themselves is a mask for lack of conjunction between power and the goods of life."[93]

Dewey seems to have changed his mind about Romantic art, which in Chapter IX is deplored as that defective kind in which

"the sense of tendencies operative beyond the limits of consummation is in excess." Romantic art, he says, "is employed to enhance
immediate appreciation, not to promote further productive achievement. . . . Excited and uneasy perceptual enjoyment is made
ultimate. . . ."[94] In Chapter IX Romantic art is said to impede progress in the same way that belief in a transcendent God, in Dewey's
opinion, does. In Chapter III he had, while admitting that "aversion
to Romanticism as a system is quite justifiable," nevertheless
praised it for "celebrating . . . something unpredictable, spontaneous, unformulable and ineffable" that "is found in any terminal
object . . . . an unpredictable and unformulable flow of immediate,
shifting, impulsive, adventured finalities, with respect to which the
universal and regular objects and principles celebrated in classic
thought are instrumental."[95]

Even if we say that he was, in the early statement, emphasizing
the evanescent finalities and, in the later, the "creation, movement"
toward higher achievement, the two attitudes toward Romantic art
cannot be reconciled. What Dewey is saying in the later statement
is that art should have a synthesis of "movement, creation, as well
as order, finality."[96] In the above passages we have one more example of Dewey's confusing use of terms—"shifting, impulsive, adventured finalities" are Romantic qualities in the first statement,
but in the second statement "finality" is a quality of Classicism[97]
synonymous with "order."

There is still an additional difference between the two passages:
it is almost as if they represented contrasting views about the destiny
of man. Following the first is this rather melancholy statement: "I
am not saying that it is a fine and noble thing that whatever is
immediately consummatory and precious should be also evanescent
and unique. . . . A reporter is not necessarily to blame for the state
of things that he reports."[98] In the later passage, art, the "culmination of nature," "involves a peculiar interpenetration of means
and ends." What is precious is not evanescent but moving toward
a higher achievement, a process repeated "in such ways as to enhance, prolong and purify the perceptual experience."[99]

VII   *"Fidelity to the Nature to Which We Belong"*

In his conclusion, Dewey refers to values rather than to art as the
"culmination of nature," but these values are attained in the same

way as is art in the previous chapter. He returns to his early emphasis on the "fugitive and precarious" quality of values—a fact which makes a theory of criticism most important. Once more criticism "implies intelligent inquiry into the conditions and consequences of a value-object," since "values are as unstable as the forms of clouds."[100] The emphasis here, as in William James's emphasis on "the constant rhythm of 'perchings and flights,' "[101] might seem to point in the direction of a refined hedonism, as in Dewey's Chapter III,[102] where he condemned the "toiling ultilitarians" who would prevent man from "taking his enjoyment neat, and at as short range as possible". But we must remember that Dewey, who never quite overcame his early love for Hegel, likes to combine opposites into a higher synthesis; he hastens to add, therefore, that "Criticism would be the most wilful of undertakings if the possession and enjoyment of good objects had no element of memory and foresight in it."[103]

Dewey warns us against the danger of "false beliefs . . . that are cherished so intolerantly and unremittingly. Beliefs about God, Nature, society, and man are precisely the things that men most cling to and most ardently fight for."[104] Dewey hopes, however, through "philosophic discourse," to disabuse our minds of the useless tendency "to delve into secrets of Being hidden from commonsense and science."[105] Common sense and science alone can give us "a heightened appreciation of the positive goods which human experience has achieved and offers."[106]

In Dewey's anxiety to avoid metaphysics and to limit himself strictly to an intelligent assessment of means-consequences, he makes, nevertheless, a sweeping statement about the "source" of values which is quite as impervious to proof as any of the statements about a transcendent Being which he rejects: "Qualitative individuality and constant relations, contingency and need, movement and arrest are common traits of all existence. This fact is source both of values and their precariousness. . . ."[107] This somewhat paradoxical argument makes nature the source because the "human situation falls wholly within nature . . . in nature itself qualities and relations, individualities and uniformities, finalities and efficacies, contingencies and necessities are inextricably bound together."[108]

Dewey certainly comes close in this concluding chapter to a mitigated form of pantheism in urging us to "fidelity to the nature to which we belong"—which will mean "converting our desires and ideals into intelligence . . . in terms of the ways and means which nature makes possible."[109] In support of his earnest exhortations he quotes the "glowing words" of Justice Holmes as an ally in insisting that man has the support of the universe, but of no Power besides it in his struggle to realize his ideals:

> That the universe has in it more than we understand, that the private soldiers have not been told the plan of campaign, or even that there is one . . . has no bearing on our conduct. We still shall fight—all of us because we want to live, some, at least, because we want to realize our spontaneity and prove our powers, for the joy of it, and we may leave to the unknown the supposed final valuation of that which in any event has value to us. . . . If we think of our existence not as that of a little god outside, but as that of a ganglion within, we have the infinite behind us. It gives us our only but our adequate significance.[110]

The reference to "private soldiers" proves that, for Holmes, there is a "General," the universe, who or which may or may not have a campaign. Nevertheless, this General is supposed to render us, if we have the proper attitude, a tremendous amount of assistance. If we think of our existence as that of "a ganglion within" the universe, "we have the infinite behind us"; and who could ask for more than that? If Holmes refers to this assistance from the infinite (the universe, that is) as a fact, he is being gravely unscientific for one who depends, as does Dewey, on the scientific method in all situations; for he cannot prove his statement. If this statement is taken on faith, it is no more convincing than faith in a transcendent God. Holmes and Dewey would answer, "We know that the universe exists: we can apprehend large parts of it with the senses." Yet they can neither know nor experimentally demonstrate that the universe "is behind us" in the sense of giving us any support besides what may well be, in its relation to man at least, cosmically accidental—sun, rain, etc.—and the statement that "we have the infinite behind us" was certainly intended to imply more than this.

So whether our support (if there is any beyond the human, and both Dewey and Holmes clearly indicate that there is) comes only from the universe or from the Creator of the universe is a question which no amount of scientific inquiry is going to prove one way or the other, even though it may be philosophically buttressed with a constant appeal to consequences. Both sides can with equal logical

Experimental Naturalism with Religious Overtones

force appeal to consequences. Both naturalists and Christian can argue that good consequences which follow the beliefs of their opponents really indicate that, in their subconscious, these believers hold the opposite view from that which they consciously express.

In spite of incidental insights that are both interesting and helpful in parts of *Experience and Nature*, the obvious conclusion would seem to be that Dewey's naturalistic argument has failed, especially in the one point which is the climax of the whole book—the semi-pantheistic concept of man's being "a ganglion within" a universe which, though without a transcendent God, guarantees that we shall "have the infinite behind us." Dewey's much desired scientific approach becomes mired in vaguely speculative philosophy. Whether the complex argument can succeed in the remaining books of this final period remains to be seen.

CHAPTER 4

Experimental Naturalism: Dewey's "Copernican Revolution" in Philosophy

I Summaries of Two Main Books

IN *Reconstruction in Philosophy* (originally published in 1920), Dewey argues that philosophy needs reconstruction for the following reason: it should be recognized that the scientific method (observation, hypothesis, and experimental test), which has been so successful in improving our material welfare, can be just as successful in solving moral and spiritual problems. Science can teach us that there should not be a separation between means and ends and that controlled change is the most important need in the world today. This view involves the denial of a realm of higher Being or fixed reality in favor of a dynamic, changing nature. This experimental change, which means progress, involves the transformation of both the experimenter and his environment. Moral and spiritual change will be more difficult than that already achieved in our physical environment, but it can be achieved when we attain enough knowledge of the scientific type. Knowledge involves an understanding of the consequences of directed operations. This understanding means that all tenets and creeds about good and goods are to be considered as hypotheses, which are to be tested by their consequences.

The Quest for Certainty (1929): Because man wishes to escape from the inevitable perils of life, philosophy has been mainly concerned with a search for the immutable. Thinking that one has found a higher realm of this type induces in the believer a quiescent dependence on it rather than on the practical effort to improve his situation as it actually exists. There is also the mistaken idea that human values must come from this putative higher realm or Being instead of being developed and improved out of one's own

57

(scientifically directed) experience. Not only ideas but idealisms are in themselves hypotheses, not finalities. It is, therefore, appropriate to be doubtful or skeptical about particular items of supposed knowledge when evidence to the contrary presents itself. There is no knowledge self-guaranteed to be infallible, for all real knowledge is the product of specially directed inquiry or activity instead of something isolated from practice. Such knowledge should guide man in restoring integration and cooperation between his beliefs about the world in which he lives and his concepts about the values and purposes that should direct his conduct.

II *Union of "Means and Ends-in-Themselves"*

Although the original edition of *Reconstruction in Philosophy* appeared in 1920, Dewey's introduction to the enlarged edition of 1948 indicates that his ideas had intensified rather than changed during the intervening years for the following reason: he says in 1948 that "Reconstruction *of* Philosophy is a more suitable title than Reconstruction *in* Philosophy." In other words, since the chaos caused by World War I had abruptly ended the preceding period of optimism and had necessitated at that time a great reconstruction of philosophy, the change demanded in 1948, when "the shock is almost incredibly greater,"[1] is proportionately intensified. But this type of reconstruction proposed by Dewey is not new; as we indicated earlier, it is the subject of one of his chapters in *Democracy and Education* (1916) and had in fact been his theme since he broke with Hegel and Christianity before the turn of the century.

To reconstruct philosophy, Dewey says in 1948 as before, "is to carry over into any inquiry into human and moral subjects the kind of method (the method of observation, theory as hypothesis, and experimental test) by which understanding of physical nature has been brought to its present pitch."[2] Such a reconstruction, he says further, "can be achieved only in terms of ends and standards so distinctively human as to constitute a new moral order."[3] As in much of his philosophy, he leaves it "for the future to undertake, even in their philosophic aspect, the specific reconstructions that are involved in this carrying to fulfillment what we have as yet attained only partially."[4] He is specific in listing only one needed reform: an end to "the divorce between mere means and ends-in-themselves, which is the theoretical correlate of the sharp division of men into free and slave, superior and inferior. Science as conducted, science in practice, has completely repudiated these separations and isolation."[5]

We may think that Christianity long ago repudiated these class distinctions and taught the dignity of all kinds of labor, but Dewey insists that such an ideal, and others which will constitute a "new moral order," can only result from the scientific method (the same kind "by which understanding of physical nature has been brought to its present pitch") applied to moral theories. If we wonder whether these theories will be put to practice since human nature is somewhat less than ideal, Dewey quotes Justice Holmes, who says in effect that "theory is the most practical thing, for good or evil, in the world."[6] If we wonder why Christian theory has not been practiced, Dewey's answer will be that it was not scientific enough, and with that statement the argument may seem to be approaching the circular.

The book which belongs most closely with *Reconstruction in Philosophy* is *Quest for Certainty* (1929).[7] The arguments are rather similar in the two, and *Quest for Certainty* ends with Dewey's supplanting Kant as the author of a real "Copernican revolution" in philosophy. If this statement seems a little brusque, we must remember that Dewey had already disposed of Kant, as well as many other philosophers of the past and present, in *Experience and Nature*. He expands on Kant's deficiencies in more detail here, and we shall examine this analysis of Kant later in this chapter.

The thesis in *Quest for Certainty* is one which is basic in Dewey's philosophy and one which he repeats many times in this book as well as in almost every other book or article that he wrote after his early break with Christianity—the denial of a realm of higher Being or fixed reality in favor of a dynamic, changing nature, all phases of which, including the spiritual, have been and are being changed for the better by the application of the principle of experimental empiricism involving the interaction between man and his environment. Because the belief in that which is antecedently real has interfered, this principle, which has been so successful in the technological part of our world, has not been widely applied to the reconstruction of our ideas about morals, economics, and politics. It would not be necessary to repeat this point in a book about Dewey except for the fact that it is central in his world view and that he approaches it from so many different angles and with so many different illustrations that a proper consideration of it eventually involves almost all the facets of his philosophy.

III   *Necessity for Scientifically Controlled Change*

Again in these two books, but more in *Reconstruction in Philosophy* than in *Quest for Certainty*, Dewey emphasizes the need for controlled change. So strong is his emphasis on change that he seems almost obsessed with it. Again and again, he stresses the importance of "the deliberate institution of a definite and specified course of change,"[8] the importance of the "development of elaborate techniques for the introduction of . . . a systematic variation of conditions so as to produce a corresponding series of changes in the thing under investigation"[9]; "the experimental method tries to break down apparent fixities and to induce changes."[10] Philosophy can "emancipate mankind from the errors which philosophy has itself fostered—the existence of conditions which are real apart from their movement into something new and different. . . ."[11] It may at times seem a little doubtful as to whether the desirable change which is to be "deliberately instituted" in a moral situation applies predominantly to the environment or to the individual self. Dewey insists always that the application of the scientific method (controlled experimentation) should apply to morals as well as to mechanical inventions, and he says that "This constant throwing of emphasis back upon a change made in ourselves instead of one made in the world in which we live seems to me the essence of what is objectionable in 'subjectivism.' "[12] He does admit that "change in personal attitude, in the disposition of the 'subject' is of great importance."[13] Yet he wants this personal change not to mean simply the contemplation of an imaginary realm of essence but to be "the means to alteration, through action, of objective conditions."[14]

Here the change in self seems to precede the change in environment; but, when Dewey argues this point against the attack of Professor Henry W. Stuart in the Schilpp volume, Dewey (apparently reversing the sequence) says: "I have indeed emphasized, in what I have said about morals, especially in their social aspects, the idea that production of new environing conditions is a prerequisite of the creation of an enduring new self."[15] This contradicts what he said not only in *Quest for Certainty* but also just two pages earlier in the Schilpp volume: "In the cognitive situation as such the overt and explicit emphasis falls upon the resolution of the situation by means of change produced in environing conditions, whereas in the distinctively moral situation it falls upon the reconstruction of the self as the distinctively demanded means."[16]

At any rate, Dewey clearly emphasizes in a moral situation the necessity for a change of the self, even to the extent in the Schilpp volume of demanding (in language suggesting a religious conversion) a "new self." He makes it clear also that this changed self is to be produced in connection with (whether before or after) "active effort which always makes some change in previous conditions—exactly as does experiment in scientific inquiry."[17] The whole analogy with experiment in scientific inquiry breaks down, however, because no moral change in the self of the experimenter is demanded in scientific inquiry. Dewey tries to make the connection by saying: "the will, the disposition, to maintain the integrity intrinsic to inquiry is a moral matter . . . . whenever the immediate problem in conduct of inquiry for the sake of obtaining knowledge involves the will to search for evidence, to weigh it fairly, not to load the dice, to control a preference for one theory over another so that it does not affect the conclusion reached, the category of truth in its *moral* sense is supreme."[18] But Dewey is loading the dice because the kind of "new self" involved in maintaining objectivity in scientific invention is very much easier than that involved in changing, for example, a long-standing habit of mistreating one's fellow man.

IV   *Relation of Scientific Knowledge and Moral Consequences*

Dewey, it is true, does recognize that the problem of creating a new self by a process exactly like "experiment in scientific inquiry" is a difficult one. "Scientific" truth requires the proper understanding of obstacles: "Of course [he says] the complexity of the conditions upon which objects of human and liberal value depend is a great obstacle, and it would be too optimistic to say that we have as yet enough knowledge of the scientific type to enable us to regulate our judgments of value very extensively. But we have more knowledge than we use, and until we try more systematically we shall not know what are the important gaps in our sciences judged from the point of view of their moral and humane use."[19]

He is always insisting upon the unfortunate dichotomy between moral theory and practice, but the main way to bridge this gap seems, in his opinion, to be to get more and more "knowledge of the scientific type." He insists that, in morality as in technology, "Experimental procedure installs doing as the heart of knowing,"[20] but how this process is to be applied to the formation of a "new self" is not very clear. Dewey seems to think that, if we really know what to do morally, we will do it. Indeed, his definition of knowledge makes this belief clear: "we know with respect to any subject-matter whatsoever in the degree in which we are able deliberately to transform doubtful situations into resolved ones."[21] He uses the word *knowledge* sometimes (as in the sentence just quoted) to mean the actual accomplishment of the desired change, and sometimes to mean the preliminary information necessary for such accomplishment. An example of the latter is the passage quoted earlier about the knowledge needed to bridge "the important gaps in our sciences judged from the point of view of their moral and humane uses."[22] The "trying," it will be noted, is for more knowledge rather than for the exertion of the moral will, which seems to be taken for granted when enough "knowledge of the scientific type" has been accumulated.

Knowledge as accomplishment, rather than preparation for accomplishment, of desired ends is also, as might be expected, a matter of consequences: indeed, "the *consequences* of directed operations form the objects that have the property of being *known*."[23] Again, as usual, Dewey makes great claims for the method of relying on consequences in deciding what the good life should be, and in evolving what he variously calls standards, principles, ideals, or values. In the new world, which he prophesies will result from following the scientific method in morals,

> all tenets and creeds about good and goods would be recognized to be hypotheses. Instead of being rigidly fixed, they would be treated as intellectual instruments to be tested and confirmed—and altered—through consequences effected by acting upon them. . . . It is both astonishing and depressing that so much of the energy of mankind has gone into fighting for (with weapons of the flesh as well as of the spirit) the truth of creeds, religious, moral and political, as distinct from what has gone into effort to try creeds by putting them to the test of acting upon them. . . . Any belief as such is tentative, hypothetical; it is not just to be acted upon, but is to be *framed* with reference to its office as a guide to action.[24]

Just how, scientifically, we can know what are the consequences of a "belief" or "creeds" Dewey never tells us; but he seems to think specific and measurable results from "acting upon them" can be ascertained. Also, he does not make clear how our own morals, for examples, are to be improved by this scientific method. If we are selfish and observe the consequences of our being so, our selfishness, or so it would seem, would distort our evaluation and, especially if we prosper materially, make us find the consequences highly desirable.[25] Dewey's answer is again in terms of consequences considered without the hindrance of belief in a transcendent God. He thinks that the world would have been much better today if "men had been systematically educated to believe that the important thing is not to get themselves personally 'right' in relation to the antecedent author and guarantor of these values, but to form their judgments and carry on their activity on the basis of public, objective and shared consequences."[26]

It never seems to have occurred to Dewey that, according to the precepts of all the great religions of the world, the only way that man can get himself personally "right" with his transcendent God (by whatever name) is to act unselfishly "on the basis of public, objective and shared consequences." Dewey admits that, on this point, his "suppositions are speculative"; and in all his work he has not traced the history of any great religion to demonstrate his assumptions about the bad effects of belief in a transcendent God.

As Professor Edward L. Schaub has said in answering Dewey's attack on such belief: "But has the belief in question as a matter of historical fact actually manifested itself as paralytic or otherwise harmful to lives of strenuous and fruitful service in the realms of thought, of art, or of social relationships? The affirmation that such has been the case would seem to depend more upon an *a priori* argument that it must have been so since the logic of the doctrine makes such a result inevitable, than to express an empirical generalization from the scroll of history."[27] As a matter of fact, Dewey himself, as late as 1908 in his *Ethics*, found much active moral good coming out of some of the great religions, especially the Hebrew and the Christian.[28] This tolerance, even praise, of such faith in a transcendent God is one inexplicable exception to Dewey's consistent denunciation of this belief after he renounced Christianity in the late 1880's.

Dewey's own religion of science and nature is emphasized again toward the end of both *Quest for Certainty* and *Reconstruction in Philosophy*—more explicitly and intellectually in the former; more lyrically and emotionally in the latter. Again, even in his most explicit argument, there is no attempt to prove (there is only the assumption) that nature, operating through its highest product, humanity, is the ultimate reality. For one who insists on the scientific method in all thinking, the following sentence seems rather weak logically: "That in fortunate moments objects of complete and approved enjoyment are had is evidence that nature is capable of giving birth to objects that stay with us as ideal."[29] Dewey would have been the first to condemn as meaningless a statement that such an experience is evidence of the presence of the Holy Spirit in the believer. But is there really any more evidence for the one than for the other? Both statements depend on faith that in such an experience the "given" comes from a source greater than the individual, and both rely on "grace": in the sentence preceding the one just quoted, Dewey refers to "the values that are enjoyed by grace in our happy moments."[30] It would be natural for the Christian to refer to the grace of God; Dewey merely says "grace," for to add "of nature or Nature" would take him closer to pantheism than he wishes to go. As he says a few pages beyond, "Nature may not be worshiped as divine even in the sense of the intellectual love of Spinoza."[31]

Dewey wants to make it clear, however, that, although he has avoided all the intellectual errors of his predecessors, he is at the same time not without heart; therefore, he immediately adds the following sentence: "But nature, including humanity, with all its defects and imperfections, may evoke heartfelt piety as the source of ideals, of possibilities, of aspiration in their behalf, and as the eventual abode of all attained goods and excellencies."[32] This statement, it must be supposed, is Dewey's version of emergent evolution, eventually attaining its own "goods and excellencies"; but the connection with the next sentence, which says that in religious experience "the sense of dependence . . . comes close to the heart of the matter,"[33] is not quite clear. It is, so it would seem, humanity that must feel this sense of dependence; but such reasoning, if we look at the preceding sentence, makes humanity feel a sense of dependence on "nature, including humanity." Apparently Dewey did not mean simply self-reliance, or he would have said so; and he did not mean to duplicate Comte's religion of humanity. The meaning, then, must remain a little foggy and, except for the already convinced naturalist, not very helpful.

V *Present and Future Identification of Religion and Art*

Although Dewey, as we have seen, intended in the above passage to exalt nature as a whole as above man, he often did exhibit an abundance, at times perhaps a superabundance, of self-reliance, as in his assertion that he, not Kant, brought about the true "Copernican revolution" in philosophy. This none too modest assumption is mistaken on two counts: first, Dewey oversimplified and therefore misunderstood Kant in the following interpretation: "Kant claimed that he had effected a Copernican revolution in philosophy by treating the world and our knowledge of it from the standpoint of the knowing subject. To most critics, the endeavor to make the known world turn on the constitution of the knowing mind, seems like a return to an ultra-Ptolemaic system. But Copernicus, as Kant understood him, effected a straightening out of astronomical phenomena by interpreting their perceived movements from their relation to the perceiving subject instead of treating them as inherent in the things perceived."[34]

It is true that Kant considered his proposal to use hypotheses about the metaphysical to be similar to Copernicus' hypothesis about the movements of the heavenly bodies. Concerning this hypothesis of Copernicus, Kant says: "the central laws of the motions of the heavenly bodies established the truth of that which Copernicus, at first, assumed only as an hypothesis, and, at the same time, brought to light the invisible force (the Newtonian attraction) which holds the universe together. The latter would have remained for ever undiscovered if Copernicus had not dared, in a manner contradictory of the senses, but yet true, to seek the observed movements, not in the heavenly bodies, but in the spectator."[35]

But Kant has not distorted Copernicus, as Norman Kemp Smith has shown by quoting [36] from Copernicus' *De Revolutionibus* the passage which clearly has the meaning that Kant claimed for it. Kemp Smith has demonstrated, furthermore, that the hypothesis of Copernicus was intended only "to achieve a more harmonious ordering of the Ptolemaic universe," and it was left for Bruno to realize later the revolutionary consequences that would develop from the new teaching.[37] But neither Copernicus nor Kant was a subjective idealist. To say, as Kant says, that the mind is so constituted that external objects conform to its organization may seem at first to make him a subjective idealist; but he devotes an important part of the Preface to the second edition of the *Critique of Pure Reason* to explaining that he has been misinterpreted on this point by some critics. He is not saying that the "world turns on the constitution of the knowing mind" but that the mind is so constituted that it can (1) know that there is something outside itself and (2) know with some degree of accuracy the nature of the external object perceived. Kant is far from saying that the characteristics of external reality depend on, and are determined by, the human mind, or that an idea in experiment is "fixed and rigorously determinative." As Kant says:

> The only addition, properly so called—and that only in the method of proof—which I have made in the present edition, consists of a new refutation of psychological *idealism*, and a strict demonstration—the only one possible, as I believe—of the objective reality of external intuition. . . . I am conscious, through internal *experience*, of my *existence in time* (consequently, also, of the determinability of the former in the latter), and that is more than the simple consciousness of my representation. It is, in fact, the same as the *empirical consciousness of my existence*, which can only be determined in relation to something, which, while connected with my existence, is *external to me*. This consciousness of my existence in time, is, therefore, identical with the consciousness of a relation to something external to me, and it is, therefore, experience, not fiction, sense, not imagination, which inseparably connects the external with my internal sense.[38]

Dewey's second error is in thinking that he himself, supplanting Kant, has brought about a truly new "Copernican revolution" in philosophy. Indeed, he gives this title to his concluding chapter in *Quest for Certainty*. He tries to clarify what he means by "sense of dependence" by saying that it "is quickened by that Copernican revolution which looks to security amid change instead of to certainty in attachment to the fixed."[39] He explains this statement by adding that "The sense of dependence that is bred by recognition that the intent and effort of man are never final but are subject to the uncertainties of an indeterminate future, would render dependence universal and shared by all."[40] This statement seems to mean that we are all in a boat that may at any time spring a leak; in this rather likely event, we must all take turns bailing out the water. But, if this is the meaning, it is hard to see how such a mixture of stoicism and brotherly love is a "Copernican revolution" in philosophy. Dewey has just been attacking pride, especially on the part of ecclesiastics who consider themselves to be superior to the secular world; but pride of whatever sort was considered to be one of the seven deadly sins long before Dewey's "revolution."

Nor do we find much more "revolutionary" light in the further explanation given by Dewey in these two sentences: "Men will never love their enemies until they cease to have enmities. The antagonism between the actual and the ideal, the spiritual and the natural, is the source of the deepest and most injurious of all enmities."[41] The first of these sentences would, however true, seem to be a commonplace; and the second (recommending a kind of Hegelian unity between the actual and the ideal) cannot be said to add anything that would introduce a new "Copernican revolution" in philosophy. Indeed, while claiming to "reconstruct philosophy," Dewey seems in most of his work to have been less original than he thought; and his reputation may finally prove to be more that of a powerful propagandist for an eclectic naturalism than that of a great innovator. In short, although he usually gave fresh and vigorous expression to the ideas of this philosophy, he was more indebted than he realized to various of his predecessors— even to some whom he condemned. As we shall see later, he also had more in common than he realized, or would admit, with some of his contemporaries, who were not his followers but, in important ways, his allies, but whom he brusquely repudiated.

Let us now try to find the supposed "Copernican revolution" in the (for Dewey) almost lyrical ending of *Reconstruction in Philosophy.* His purpose here is not merely the ethical transformation of the individual into a "new self" (which, he assured his critics in the Schilpp volume, was implicit in his philosophy) but the transformation of all society. In short, he promises those who follow his philosophy that they will be "expediting the development of the vital sources of a religion and art that are yet to be."[42] It may be noted that he equates "religion and art," a combination which becomes clearer when we examine *Art as Experience.* That art is the senior partner in this firm, however, may be seen in the description of the Deweyan millennium, "the progress, free movement and infinitely diversified opportunity" of which "have been suggested by modern science":[43]

> When the liberation of capacity no longer seems a menace to organization and established institutions, something that cannot be avoided practically and yet something that is a threat to conservation of the

67

most precious values of the past, when the liberating of human capacity operates as a socially creative force, art will not be a luxury, a stranger to the daily occupations of making a living. . . . And when the emotional force, the mystic force one might say, of communication, of the miracle of shared life and shared experience is spontaneously felt, the hardness and crudeness of contemporary life will be bathed in the light that never was on land or sea.[44]

Indeed, in this statement—Dewey's version of a Romantic religion (with the quotation from Wordsworth and the overtones of a secularized Isaiah)—we have the identification of art (broadly defined) and religion with science as the voice crying in the wilderness. The new religion will go beyond experimental science to "a spontaneous way of envisaging life. . . ideas . . . spontaneously fed by emotion. . . shared experience spontaneously felt."[45] The step from experimental science to this marvelous spontaneity, however, is never made clear; but Dewey attempts clarification by saying that "The religious spirit will be revivified because it will be in harmony with men's unquestioned scientific beliefs and their ordinary day-by-day activities."[46] Perhaps he could have made the transition more convincing if he had made more of the unconscious, which he mentions twice within two pages as a reinforcement for the new religion ("ideas and beliefs . . . unconsciously transmitted and sustained" and "thoughts and desires that unconsciously converge . . ."[47]); but which he never develops, after the manner of the psychoanalysts, into its scientific (psychological) ramifications. Indeed, Dewey had in *Experience and Nature* found certain dangers in living by the subconscious. He believed in its usefulness as intuition in "mathematics or philosophizing far away from concrete situations, or in a highly cultivated fine art," but he warned against dependence on the subconscious in any form "in connection with intimate matters of self-regulation in health, morals, social affairs—in matters most closely connected with basic needs and relationships."[48]

The romantically religious Dewey appears in two other books discussed in detail in the next two chapters—*A Common Faith* and *Art as Experience* (both of which appeared in 1934).

CHAPTER 5

Experimental Naturalism as Religion: "Natural Piety" and "Poetic Pantheism" Fully Developed

I *Summary of* A Common Faith

THE religious attitude can and should be emancipated from formal or institutional religion because all religions "convert the idealism of action into a system of beliefs about antecedent reality." Such a belief that the ideal already exists in some immutable realm induces in the believer a quiescent and superstitious dependence on a static supernatural rather than an active determination to improve himself and his environment. The word *God* may be effectively used so long as it means no more than "a working union of the ideal and the actual" or a concept of "ideal possibilities unified through imaginative realization and projection." This is not to say that man is completely dependent on himself because there are "factors in existence that generate and support our idea of good as an end to be striven for." Indeed, it may be said that "Nature produces whatever gives reinforcement and direction but also what occasions discord and confusion." This approach to Nature means emergence and growth, which must be accompanied by toil and, at times, pain. The potential significance of this cooperation between man and Nature is infinite.

The scientific method, construed in its most generous and general sense, should be applied to the discovery of what is true about religious beliefs. This open and public method of intelligence should be opposed to the limited, private, and therefore undependable doctrinal method. The objects of religion are ideal in contrast with our present state, but this fact does not mean that they already exist in some eternal realm of Being. The aims and ideals that most effectively move us are generated through human imagination, and they are made from the stuff of the world of physical and social experience.

A religion based on the supernatural mistakenly draws a line between the religious and the secular and profane, and it substitutes the authority of the church for individual responsibility. The church as a formal institution has become an agent that hinders true social progress and the application of the method of natural intelligence. Social evils must not be disposed of as due to man's sinful nature; their complex underlying causes must be analyzed and then solved by the application of the scientific method. Only in this way can the influence of vested interests now dominating the church and the rest of society be overcome.

II   *Harmonizing of Self with Universe*

Dewey's most prolonged and specific discussion of his attitude toward religion is the short book (summarized above) entitled *A Common Faith* (1934) based upon his Terry Lectures at Yale. This book, the eleventh in the series of "Lectures on Religion in the Light of Science and Philosophy," proved to be very popular; it went through thirteen printings by 1957. One reason for the popularity of the book is that it is written in Dewey's clearest and least technical style,—one which avoids, for the most part, the tortuous subtleties that characterize much of his writing. It has also been popular because Dewey restores the word "God" to his religious vocabulary and thus reassures those who had been disturbed by its omission since he had renounced Christianity in the 1880's. This concession (however slight when its real meaning is understood) to theism has been comforting to some who really believe in God and to all those for whom the word "God" provides (in the words of I. A. Richards) "emotional therapy" without belief. It is also comforting to some to be told that one can be "religious" (and that it is really preferable to be so) without having a "religion."

Dewey wants to "emancipate the religious from religion,"[1] because all religions

> convert the idealism of action into a system of beliefs about antecedent reality. The character assigned this reality is so different from that which observation and reflection lead to and support that these schemes inevitably glide into alliance with the supernatural.

> All religions, marked by elevated ideal quality, have dwelt upon the power of religion to introduce perspective into the piecemeal and shift-

ting episodes of existence. Here too we need to reverse the ordinary
statement and say that whatever introduces genuine perspective is
religious, not that religion is something that introduces it.[2]

Dewey does, however, finally decide to allow the use of the word
"God" to denote "a working union of the ideal and the actual"; and
his main reasons for this concession are (1) that "aggressive atheism
seems to me to have something in common with traditional supernaturalism,"[3] and (2) "Use of the words 'God' or 'divine' to convey
the union of actual with ideal may protect man from a sense of isolation and from consequent despair or defiance."[4]

Although Dewey's idea of God is "one of ideal possibilities unified
through imaginative realization and projection,"[5] his concept also
has an objective aspect since "there are forces in nature and society
that generate and support the ideals."[6] These forces in nature (sometimes he calls them simply "Nature" or "mother nature") form the
basis of the religion which Dewey claimed for himself in an interview in 1941 with Max Eastman (part of which has been already
quoted—see above, Chapter l, pp. 13-14). Dewey claimed that he
had had this religion ever since an early, somewhat mystical experience when he was a young high-school teacher in Oil City, Pennsylvania, 1879. He described it as similar "to the poetic pantheism of
Wordsworth, whom he was reading at the time, and to Walt Whitman's sense of oneness with the universe." If Dewey had been
accused of contradiction between his statement that he had a religion similar to poetic pantheism and his condemnation of religions
of all kinds in *A Common Faith*, he would have probably answered,
with some justification, that what he really had was not a *religion*
but a *religious* attitude. This same religion, or religious attitude, he
had described in several places in *Experience and Nature*, especially
in the long quotation from Justice Holmes about the universe as a
general in the cosmic army and the individual as a private—a rela-
tionship which, properly understood, gives us the justified feeling
that "we have the infinite behind us."

That Dewey's "natural piety" involves a kind of worship is clearly
indicated in the following passage from *A Common Faith*: "For it
[his idea of "God" or "divine"] involves no miscellaneous worship
of everything in general. It selects those factors in existence that
generate and support our idea of good as an end to be striven for. It
excludes a multitude of forces that at any given time are irrelevant
to this function. Nature produces whatever gives reinforcement and

direction but also what occasions discord and confusion. The 'divine' is thus a term of human choice and aspiration."[7] We have already quoted part of this passage to indicate that, in it at least, Dewey considers certain aspects of nature to be superior to man, to be even worthy of worship by man, since these "factors in existence" which he selects for worship "generate and support our idea of good." Here, then, he is approaching the limited pantheism (Dewey called it "poetic pantheism") which is, intermittently, part of his religious attitude.

It may be objected that Dewey is not a pantheist since his idea of the "divine" is limited to "human choice" which "selects" for worship "those factors in existence that generate and support our idea of good . . ."; and, of course, it is true that, even in part of *A Common Faith*, man is emphasized so much that naturalistic humanism seems to be the religion indicated. But Dewey's emphasis alternates (if not vacillates) between exaltation of man and exaltation of nature as greater than man; and, when, as frequently happens, he is in the latter mood, he approaches that mitigated form of pantheism described by Professor John Laird: "Deity is held to be dia-cosmic, not hyper-cosmic, and the cosmos is taken to mean the world, astronomical, biological, and human. The theory is a theory of *Natura sive Deus*, but not of a Godless nature; for it holds that nature is deiform although it also holds (being but a mitigated pantheism) that nature contains much evil and much else that cannot, obviously and directly, be called divine."[8]

This is the kind of religion implied when Dewey says, in explaining his idea of "God" or the "divine," that "Nature produces whatever gives reinforcement and direction but also what occasions discord and confusion." Thus Dewey would carefully select what Professor Laird calls the "deiform" aspects for purposes of worship but omit the great amount of natural "evil and much else that cannot, obviously and directly, be called divine." That Dewey's concept of the "divine," though "a term of human choice and aspiration," is at this point not limited to man, either individual or collective, is further indicated by the following statement: "A humanistic religion, if it excludes our relation to nature, is pale and thin, as it is presumptuous when it takes humanity as an object of worship."[9]

But Dewey admittedly has some logical difficulties in doing homage to a nature that is what he metaphorically calls a good "mother," who often changes into an evil "stepmother." For one thing, this badly mixed metaphor obviously cannot bear logical analysis except at the fairy-tale level of magical transformation if nature, in terms of the metaphor, shifts from one role to the other. But more serious than the faulty metaphor is the logical dilemma represented by the metaphor. Which is the real nature, the good or the bad; and is it not more logical to assume that nature should be given neither credit for the good nor blame for the evil, but that cosmically both are accidental? Christian theology has difficulties with the problem of natural evil, but these questions can be convincingly answered in the Christian doctrine of a transcendent but benevolent and even suffering God. (See the works of Professors John Hick and Ian Crombie for intelligent discussions of this point.)[10]

Since Dewey can rely only on nature beyond man, he has a tendency to mention in passing but not to stress those natural phenomena which made John Stuart Mill say[11] that much of man's progress has been made in spite of, not through the assistance of, nature, which (in the various phases of natural catastrophes and disease) can be more cruel than the cruelest human tyrant has ever been. Dewey, as a naturalist wishing to display fully his "natural piety," never really wrestles with such problems; instead, he quotes the historian James Henry Breasted, who says that "nature has been friendly to the emergence and development of conscience and character."[12] Dewey attempts to dispose of all objections to this idea that nature is benevolent by saying, apparently in defense of a non— "mechanicalized" [Dewey's term] nature, that "Those who will have all or nothing cannot be satisfied with this answer. Emergence and growth are not enough for them. They want something more than growth accompanied by toil and pain. They want final achievement."[13]

But, if we look at the superlatives which Dewey uses to prophesy the results of the elimination of "supernatural religions" and the eventual adoption of his system, it seems that he, too, expects final achievement, or infinite growth. For example, he states that "the potential religious significance of this fact [that we are "all in the same boat traversing the same turbulent ocean"] is infinite."[14] Indeed, Christianity (though Dewey seems unaware of this fact) has from the very first insisted that growth must be accompanied by toil and pain. Saint Paul speaks of continual creation as a tremen-

73

dous process in which "the whole creation groaneth and travaileth," and Teilhard de Chardin refers to the Kingdom of God as, in one sense, "a prodigious biological operation—that of the Redeeming Incarnation."[15]

The big difference between Christianity and Dewey's system is that his God is limited to the projection of man's ideals and his Nature is sometimes limited (sometimes not) to "those factors in existence that generate and support our idea of good as an end to be striven for,"[16] while the Christian God is the transcendent, all-wise, benevolent Creator. If we think that Dewey's God, like some of the pagan gods, may be rather ineffectual in a crisis, we must remember that Dewey agrees with Justice Holmes's statement (quoted above) that "we have the infinite behind us."[17] But believers in a transcendent God (and there are some) who claim Dewey as an ally must be disappointed when they recall that the "infinite" on which Holmes and Dewey are relying is synonymous with the universe, not with its Creator.

III *"Stability and Peace in Matrix of Human Relations"*

So far in this chapter Dewey has seemed to rely mainly, as he did in *Experience and Nature,* on Nature as our mother, through whose bounty we have the "infinite behind us." But even in this reliance the child sometimes seems to be more important than the mother; indeed, in passages like the following the relations are mainly those among people rather than between people and nature; of course, nature is there in the form of "natural goods," on which "an idealizing imagination has laid hold" so that "values" are "produced." The definite emphasis, however, rather than being on "the infinite behind us," is on the fact "that all significant ends and all securities for stability and peace have grown up in the matrix of *human* [italics mine] relations. . . ."[18] Indeed, the title of his last chapter is "The Human Abode of the Religious Function."

In attacking religions that worship a transcendent God, Dewey again makes charges which are absurdly exaggerated and which he, rather noticeably for one so insistent on scientific method, never attempts to document. "Natural relations, of husband and wife," he says, "of parent and child, friend and friend, neighbor and neighbor, of fellow workers in industry, science, and art are . . . not merely depreciated. They have been regarded as dangerous rivals of higher values; as offering temptations to be resisted; as usurpations by flesh of the authority of the spirit; as revolts of the human against the divine."[19] It need hardly be pointed out that Dewey is taking as typical of Christianity what applies only to a small number of saints, none of whom considered these relationships "dangerous rivals of higher values" for the many not called to a celibate and/or monastic type of religious life.

Dewey admits that "The values found in natural and supernatural relationships are now, in liberal circles, said to be complementary, just as the truths of revelation and of science are the two sides, mutually sustaining, of the same ultimate truth."[20] What he does not realize is that Saint Thomas Aquinas long ago denied the conflict between natural science and revelation.[21]

Dewey says that "vested interests, interests vested with power, are powerfully on the side of the *status quo*, and therefore they are especially powerful in hindering the growth and application of the method of natural intelligence."[22] Of course, he is correct in saying that there are vested interests on the side of the status quo, but the looseness of his language is evident in his saying that they are "hindering the growth and application of the method of natural intelligence." The truth is that they are using with great skill *a* method of natural intelligence in maintaining their position, and they are at the same time prime examples of "The sinfulness of man, the corruption of his heart, his self-love and love of power," which Dewey denies as causes of the present social evils. Reference to such moral causes, says Dewey, is one of the "chief obstacles" in combatting social evils—comparable, he adds, to appealing to demons in order to explain bodily disease.

In spite of his generally optimistic attitude toward human nature and his argument that morality has suffered because it "set up rules so foreign to human nature," which has been shamefully "blackened by theologians who have thought to honor the divine by disparaging the human,"[23] Dewey recognizes the many evils existing in the twentieth century especially during and after World War I; but he still insists, as he did then, that human nature is not to blame. In *Human Nature and Conduct* he had used the same argument:

> Moral principles that exalt themselves by degrading human nature are in effect committing suicide. Or else they involve human nature in unending civil war, and treat it as a hopeless mess of contradictory forces.
>   We are forced therefore to consider the nature and origin of that control of human nature with which morals has been occupied. And the

fact which is forced upon us when we raise this question is the existence of classes. Control has been vested in an oligarchy. . . . Parents, priests, chiefs, social censors have supplied aims, aims which were foreign to those upon whom they were imposed. . . . Generally speaking, good people have been those who did what they were told to do, and lack of eager compliance is a sign of something wrong in their nature.[24]

This passage might be considered as leaning toward the Marxist analysis of society, with an admixture of Rousseauism in the inclusion of parents as tyrants oppressing their children. Of course, Dewey and the Marxists are correct in referring to the existence of classes (the upper oppressing the lower); but this condition is strong evidence of the evil in human nature which Dewey is denying, and it has all too frequently proved true that, when such conditions proved intolerable and resulted in revolution, the succeeding rulers were quite as oppressive as those whom they succeeded. We do not deny the necessity of revolution when or even before evils become intolerable, and we may agree with Dewey and Jefferson that we must have democracy; but we need it, not because human nature is (as they thought) usually good, but because it easily becomes bad. The very vital provision of checks and balances in the American Constitution, for example, is necessary to prevent factions from getting control and imposing their will on the rest of the country.

IV *Belief in Transcendent God Impediment to Moral Progress*

We need Christianity for the same reason, and Dewey has never been more unrealistic than in the following passage, which may be called the Apostles' Creed of his secular, "scientific" religion: "One of the few experiments in the attachment of emotion to ends that mankind has not tried is that of devotion, so intense as to be religious, to intelligence as a force in social action."[25] This devotion, so he says, is to be achieved without belief in a transcendent God; indeed, such a belief is an actual hindrance in reaching this goal. With this hindrance removed (shades of the youthful Shelley again!), mankind could experience "the intense realization of values that inhere in the actual connections of human beings with one another."[26] Dewey would welcome the participation of churches in this great movement, if they would only give up their stultifying belief in a transcendent God. Historic Christianity, laments Dewey, "has been committed to a separation of sheep and goats; the saved and the lost; the elect and the mass."[27] Dewey would remove this division and recognize that we are "all in the same boat traversing the same turbulent ocean. The potential religious significance of this fact is infinite."[28]

Statements like these are so much like a fundamental tenet of Christianity, the brotherhood of man, that some critics have actually interpreted Dewey as either already Christian[29] or as on the verge of Christianity;[30] but what they forget is that Dewey considered statements like the one just quoted as sharply differentiating him from Christianity with its superstitious belief in a transcendent God and its "separation of sheep and goats. . . ." Dependence on such a God, for Dewey, is the chief obstacle in reaching this goal of the brotherhood of man, which, in his version, conspicuously lacks the fatherhood of God. It is also to be noted that in this final chapter, with its emphasis on "The Human Abode of the Religious Function," Dewey does not say much about the motherhood of nature. He is here in one of his strongly humanistic moods in which parental control of whatever type (beyond the human) is considered a hindrance to the realization of the goal, which remains "infinite,"[31] but only in the sense of a tremendous extension of human goodness activated by its own potential "divinity."

Toward the end of *A Common Faith* he perhaps restores the pre-eminence to Nature by referring to it as "the mysterious totality of being the imagination calls the universe," though the language is ambiguous: "Nature," he explains further, "is the embodiment for sense and thought of that encompassing scope of existence the intellect cannot grasp. It is the matrix within which our ideal aspirations are born and bred. It is the source of the values that the moral imagination projects as directive criteria and as shaping purposes."[32]

This hovering between the human and the more than human (but not more than nature) centers in "the mysterious totality of being the imagination calls the universe." If the emphasis is on the imagination, then the human image maker is more important than the imagined "totality of being." If the image maker is, even though vaguely through his images, recognizing something superior to himself, then we have a different emphasis—on "that encompassing scope of existence the intellect cannot grasp," or on "the matrix within which our ideal aspirations are born and bred." We seem to continue this emphasis into the next sentence when this same "totality of being the imagination calls the universe" is called "the source of our values," but the emphasis abruptly shifts back to the human when these values are said to be "projected by the moral [human] imagination as directive criteria and as shaping purposes."

All thinking Christians will be ready to join with Dewey in his striving for ideal ends, but they will disagree sharply with his belief (and for all his talk of experimental testing of his theory, it is only a belief) that dependence on a transcendent God is a hindrance in this great struggle. They will remind his devoted followers, many of whom are still with us, that the master himself did not always feel this way about Christianity and the Hebraic religion from which it descended. "Certain periods in history," he said as late as 1908 in his *Ethics*, "have transferred the ideal entirely to another world, regarding human society as hopelessly given over to evil. Such theories find a morality possible only by renouncing society. The Hebrews presented rather the ideal of a moral order on earth. . . . It was an ideal not dreamed out in ecstatic visions of pure fancy, but worked out in struggle and suffering, in confidence that moral efforts are not hopeless or destined to defeat. The ideal order is to be made real. The divine kingdom is to come, the divine will to be done '*on earth* as it is in heaven.' "[33]

6

Romanticism: The Transformation of the World Through Art

IN spite of the fact that the world is full of pain and constantly threatened with disorder, Dewey makes clear in *Art as Experience* that all is for the best since resistance and tension enable the artist to bring to living consciousness an experience that is unified and total. Such an experience of a harmonious whole is a kind of religious feeling which makes us feel that we are citizens of a vast world beyond ourselves. This experience, which accompanies intense esthetic perception, is partly the result of man's own synthesizing imagination and also part of the process of nature which "becomes conscious with man."

Part of nature's great unifying plan may be learned from observation (and, to some extent, imitation) of the alert and unified activities of lower animals. Works of art are marvelous aids in the creation of a unified collective life. Art at its best is the culmination of nature and produces in us a happy transfiguration of appetites and transformation of emotion. Even though art is to be distinguished from propositional statements, it is closely related to life since it presents a thorough and complete interpenetration of the material of undergoing and of action, including a reorganization of past experience.

Art should remain close to nature and should contain a symmetry and rhythm like those found in nature. The art experience for the artist should begin with "a total seizure, an inclusive qualitative whole not yet articulated"; and, even after distinctions emerge, the artist should feel, and eventually convey to the observer, a somewhat mystical relation to "the indefinite total setting" or "unlimited envelope." Such feeling can prepare the way for the "wide and large redirections of desire and purpose" and for the transformation of civilization which art will eventually accomplish.

I *"The Deep-seated Memory of Underlying Harmony"*

Throughout *Art as Experience* Dewey has as his theme the idea (first formulated in *Experience and Nature*) that art is "the complete culmination of nature" and that science is "properly a handmaiden that conducts events to this happy issue."[1] Indeed, he makes art a kind of panacea for all the ills of mankind. Yet his exaggerated claims for art alternate with some very intelligent and appropriate comments about the importance of making art a part of the daily life of all the people and of overcoming the separation between the useful and the fine arts.

Indeed, Dewey makes a laudable attempt to extend the concept of the esthetic to include any integral or unified experience. "The most elaborate philosophical or scientific inquiry and the most ambitious industrial or political enterprise," he says, "has, when its different ingredients constitute an integral experience, esthetic quality," but such experiences "are dominantly intellectual or practical, rather than *distinctively* esthetic," the latter type being "an integrated complete experience on its own account."[2] The parts of *Art as Experience* in which Dewey fails are those in which he attempts to interpret all of life as one great esthetic whole or to find in art the salvation of the world—a claim quite as extravagant as the substitution of poetry for religion by the French Symbolists in the nineteenth century, though Dewey's esthetics differs in most ways from their estheticism.

His first chapter is a curious and contradictory combination of various comments which vacillate between praise of this world as the best of all possible worlds and admission that it is "full of pain."[3] Even the pain, however, he tried to weave into the great esthetic whole as part of the rhythm of what Havelock Ellis would have called "The Dance of Life."[4] "The world," Dewey admits, "is full of things that are indifferent and even hostile to life; the very processes by which life is maintained tend to throw it out of gear with its surroundings. . . . Equilibrium comes about not mechanically and inertly but out of, and because of, tension."[5] So, in spite of the fact that the world is "full of pain" and "constantly threatened with disorder," all is for the best; for the esthetic whole would not be possible without "the rhythm of loss of integration with environment and recovery of union. . . ." Indeed, the artist "does not shun moments of resistance and tension. He rather cultivates them, not for their own sake but because of their potentialities, bringing to living consciousness an experience that is unified and total."[6]

Since Dewey is referring to all of life and attempting to bring it into a harmonious whole, we might find an analogy with Saint Thomas Aquinas' attempt to dispose of the problem of evil by saying that God permits it only because He can and does bring good out of it. The obvious difference is that, in Dewey's world view, the equilibrium "is not imposed from without"[7] but develops in and through nature only; and this wonderful "rhythm" (which includes all the evils of the world, both moral and natural, and the "recovery" from them) "not only persists in man but becomes conscious with him."[8] Dewey does not intend to include "destruction and death" in the "ordered change" which constitutes life; but even from these, he says, "new rhythms are built up . . . through the phases of perturbation and conflict, there abides the deep-seated memory of an underlying harmony, the sense of which haunts life like the sense of being founded on a rock."[9]

This trust in the "underlying harmony" provided for us by "mother" nature is somewhat like that of Santayana and Emerson, who say that what we think is a natural catastrophe is really only nature's manner of concealing from us for a time the good that she has planned for us a little later. As Emerson says: "To offset the drag of temperament and race, which pulls down, learn this lesson, namely, that by the cunning copresence of two elements, which is throughout nature, whatever lames or paralyzes you draws in with it the divinity, in some form, to repay."[10] However, Dewey expresses more emphatically than do Santayana and Emerson the ambivalent aspects of nature by saying that "Nature is the mother and the habitat of man, even if sometimes a step-mother and an unfriendly home."[11]

Professor James Collins says that Dewey started out with a psychological idealism (derived from Hegel's logic of the absolute idea) but soon abandoned his "idealistic conception of the totality of consciousness" in favor of "experience and philosophical method in terms of a natural reality given fundamentally through the empirical sciences. . . ."[12] Such naturalism, adds Professor Collins, involves "a withdrawal of respect for ultimate explanations, fixed structures and universal purposes, so that men can concentrate upon nature in its particular phases, its fluent qualities, and its capacity for limited aims and satisfactions."[13]

But the fact remains that scattered through Dewey's later writings (along with a concentration on its particular phases) are, as in this book, references to this great harmonious whole, this wonderful "religious feeling" which "raises to great clarity" the "sense of an enveloping undefined whole" and which makes us "citizens of this vast world beyond ourselves."[14] This mystical experience ("the religious feeling that accompanies intense esthetic perception"[15]) is partly the result of man's own synthesizing imagination, but it is also part of the process of nature which "becomes conscious with" man. Man is nature become intelligent, and nature is in a way an ultimate explanation as may be seen in Dewey's quotation with approval (in *Experience and Nature*) of Justice Holmes's famous passage relating man to the cosmos as a private soldier to a rather puzzling but awesome general, whose plans (if he has any) we cannot understand. If we follow this general or if we (changing the metaphor) consider ourselves humbly as "a ganglion within" the great nerve structure of the universe, we will have the "joy" of knowing that "we have the infinite behind us."[16]

II *Superman Inspired by the Primitive*

Part of nature's great unifying plan, says Dewey (shifting to a kind of primitivistic mood), may be learned from observation (and, to some extent, imitation) of lower animals: "The activities of the fox, the dog, and the thrush may at least stand as reminders and symbols of that unity of experience which we so fractionize when work is labor, and thought withdraws us from the world." For the live animal, "All senses are equally on the *qui vive*." We can also learn something from the savage, who "is as active through his whole being when he looks and listens as when he stalks his quarry or stealthily retreats from a foe."[17]

In *Art and Experience*, as in his other books, Dewey usually considers nature as superior to man—an attitude of "Natural piety" or "poetic pantheism," to use again Dewey's own words[18] describing his religion. At times, however, man assumes control in the spirit of Romanticists such as Keats and Shelley, from both of whom, especially Keats, Dewey quotes extensively in *Art and Experience*. For example, the inspiration for this second chapter, entitled "The Live Creature and 'Etherial Things,'" comes from the following quotation from Keats: "The Sun, the Moon, the Earth and its contents, are material to form greater things, that is, etherial things—

greater things than the Creator himself made."[19] This wonderful
life of the Deweyan superman will begin, he thinks, when there are
no longer "Oppositions of mind and body, soul and matter, spirit
and flesh," when "What is distinctive in man makes it possible for
him . . . to carry to new and unprecedented heights that unity of
sense and impulse, of brain and eye and ear, that is exemplified
in animal life, saturating it with the conscious meanings derived
from communication and deliberate expression."[20]

As the "culmination of nature," art will be the main force enabling man to reach these "new and unprecedented heights." Works
of art are "marvelous aids in the creation of a unified collective
life," in which "an infinitely greater happiness than is now the case
would attend all modes of production."[21] Indeed, art in a way already brings us a kind of heaven on earth—a "transfiguration" of
appetites and a "transformation" of emotion: "Expression in art
is the clarification of turbid emotion; our appetites know themselves
when they are reflected in the mirror of art, and as they know themselves they are transfigured. Emotion that is distinctively esthetic
then occurs . . . natural emotions that have been transformed."[22]
Dewey seems to mean more here even than Wordworth's "emotion
recollected in tranquility," for in Dewey's prophecy, since art "is
more moral than moralities,"[23] it will also transform society. As the
"culmination of nature," then, art is the messiah for this version of
Dewey's secular religion of science and nature.

III *Art as Coalescence of Emotion and Intellect*

If we look merely at Dewey's comments on the nature of art,
ignoring the tremendous effect that he thinks it has had and will
have in the transformation of society, we can agree with most of
what he says. His views avoid the extremes of all the theories that
tend to "separate the live creature from the world in which it
lives."[24] He distinguishes art, however, from propositional statements. For example, "The logic of poetry is superpropositional
even when it uses what are, grammatically speaking, propositions.
The latter have intent; art is an immediate realization of intent."[25]
He cannot agree with Roger Fry, however, that there is "a radical
difference between esthetic values that are intrinsic to things of
ordinary experience and the esthetic value with which the artist
is concerned."[26]

Dewey agrees with Dr. A. C. Barnes that abstract art may be

valuable "as a paradigm of the visible essence of all things," which "may hold in solution the emotions which individualized things provoke in a more specialized way."[27] But Dewey warns that in abstract art "The one limit that must not be overpassed is that some reference to the qualities and structure of things in environment remain."[28] In art he wants a unified whole composed of "direct sensuous matter and that which is incorporated with it because of prior experience."[29] His definition of the complete art experience is almost precisely that which he gives in *Experience and Nature* for any kind of complete experience: "The expressiveness of the object of art is due to the fact that it presents a thorough and complete interpenetration of the material of undergoing and of action, the latter including a reorganization of matter brought with us from past experience."[30]

Dewey believes also that form and matter are connected in a work of art, but they are not identical. The work, he says, is "formed matter."[31] The sensuous qualities and the intellectual properties of an object of art must coalesce. All reference to T. S. Eliot's having made this same point concerning the poetry of John Donne is noticeably absent from Dewey's discussion. He quotes instead the prose works of Keats, Shelley, and Wordsworth more than those of any other writers on esthetic theory, and he makes extended reference to Kant's *Critique of Judgement* as his main example of a defective theory. He also quotes the poetry of Wordsworth and Keats in several instances to illustrate a point. For example, two stanzas from "Lucy Gray" are quoted[32] to illustrate the integration of sense and thought. The point is well made, and the quotation of Keats's "casements opening on the foam/ Of perilous seas in faery lands forlorn" (with the strange omission of "Charmed magic" at the beginning of the first line) may serve to illustrate how art "keeps alive the power to experience the common world in its fullness,"[33] but it is not clear how these famous passages, though multiplied many times by examples from all the fine arts, "institute wide and large redirections of desire and purpose . . ."[34] and transform civilization.

IV   *Art Making "Grand Democracy of Forest Trees!"*

Professor Stephen Pepper has called *Art as Experience* a "confused book"[35] because it presents, without reconciling them, two esthetic theories that contradict each other—the "pragmatic" and

84

the "organicist." The former, he says, is "a theory of conflict, celebrating struggle and vigorous life in which every solution is the beginning of a new problem. . . ."[36] The latter "is a theory of harmony
culminating in the great cosmic harmony of the absolute."[37] Pepper
quotes the following sentence from *Art as Experience* as an example
of "organicism": "This sense of the including whole implicit in
ordinary experience is rendered intense within the frame of a
painting or poem. It, rather than any special purgation, is that which
reconciles us to the events of tragedy."[38] Dewey answers this argument by saying that he uses *whole, integration, complete,* not to
refer to the "great cosmic harmony of the absolute," but to refer
only to "a consummatory appreciation of material or an individual
qualitative experience."[39]

But the sum total of the "consummatory appreciations" will
eventually, in Dewey's opinion, make of civilization a kind of ideal
state—an artistic, and eventually a political, paradise, in which
every man (he quotes from Keats), "filling the air with a beautiful
circuiting . . . should not dispute or assert, but whisper results to
his neighbor, and thus, by every germ of spirit sucking the sap from
mold ethereal, every human being might become great, and
Humanity instead of being a wide heath of Furze and briars with
here and there a remote Pine or Oak, would become a grand democracy of Forest Trees!"[40]

Is this utopian vision really very different from "the great cosmic
harmony of the absolute" prophesied for art in the organicist
theory? Perhaps Dewey could argue that "a grand democracy of
Forest Trees" is limited to earth and is not to be construed as a
cosmic absolute, but the extravagance of the claims made in each
of these theories (if they are indeed different from each other)
makes them variations of Romanticism, whether the art experience
be approached first by a "seizure" (Dewey's word) or by the intellectual plans of the careful craftsman.

Dewey, as might be expected, wants art to remain close to nature,
especially since it is true that rhythms are fundamental to each: "naturalism in the broadest and deepest sense of nature is a necessity of
all great art, even of the most religiously conventional and of abstract painting, and of the drama that deals with human action in an
urban setting. Discrimination can be made only with reference to
the particular aspect and phase of nature in which the rhythms that
mark all relationships of life and its setting are displayed."[41]

Dewey emphasizes the relation of rhythm thus broadly defined to symmetry. "Symmetry and rhythm," he says, "are the same thing felt with the difference of emphasis that is due to attentive interest. When intervals that define rest and relative fulfillment are the traits that especially characterize perception, we are aware of symmetry. When we are concerned with movement, with comings and goings rather than arrivals, rhythm stands out. But in every case, symmetry, since it is the equilibrium of counteracting energies, involves rhythm, while rhythm occurs only when movement is spaced by places of rest, and hence involves measure."[42]

In the chapter "The Common Substance of the Arts," Dewey resumes a favorite theme: the importance of the removal of "an invidious distinction,"[43] both in form and in substance, between the fine and the useful arts. He discusses also the progress of the individual art experience for both artist and perceiver. Such experience begins, he says, with "a total seizure, an inclusive qualitative whole not yet articulated,"[44] which "persists as the substratum after distinctions emerge."[45] This "seizure" idea Professor Pepper considers a part of the pragmatic theory of esthetics. Dewey goes beyond this idea to what Professor Pepper calls the organicist theory and what we call the Romantic theory of "the indefinite total setting"[46] or "unlimited envelope." "There is," says Dewey, "something mystical associated with the word intuition, and any experience becomes mystical in the degree in which the sense, the feeling, of the unlimited envelope becomes intense—as it may do in experience of an object of art. . . . The sense of the including whole implicit in ordinary experiences is rendered intense within the frame of a painting or poem."[47]

It is hard to see how Dewey can argue here, as he does in answer to Professor Pepper's argument, that he intends no more than "a consummatory appreciation of material of an individual qualitative experience" when he refers to "the indefinite total setting" and the "unlimited envelope" of the art experience. Dewey may maintain with some justification that these "mystical" phases do not refer to "the great cosmic harmony of the absolute," but "the feeling of the unlimited envelope . . . in experience of an object of art" must certainly prepare the way for the "wide and large redirections of desire and purpose"[48] and the transformation of civilization which in his last chapter he says art will accomplish.

In the chapter "The Varied Substance of the Arts" he also very explicitly stresses the "miracle" achieved by art. As "communication in its pure and undefiled form, art breaks through barriers that divide human beings, which are impermeable in ordinary association."[49] As might be expected, Dewey then attacks the eighteenth-century and Kantian idea of art as primarily contemplative, as concerned with "reason" rather than with "passion"—so that "objective order and regularity, the invariant element, was almost exclusively the source of esthetic satisfaction."[50] He repeats his reasonable contention that the art experience should produce "an integral union of sense quality and meaning in a single firm texture . . . . Art has the faculty of enhancing and concentrating this union of quality and meaning in a way which vivifies both."[51]

But Dewey lapses again into Romantic extravagance when he makes art the culmination of religion in a way that the French Symbolists would have applauded. We should consider, for example, the following passage: "Art is the *extension* [italics mine] of the power of rites and ceremonies to unite men, through a shared celebration, to all incidents and scenes of life. This office is the reward of art. . . . Art renders men aware of their union with one another in origin and destiny."[52]

V *"Esthetic Experience Ineffable and Mystical"*

By apparent contrast with the above claim that art is the all-inclusive culmination of religion, Dewey might seem to be limiting the claims made by some philosophers for art when he objects to Aristotle's statement that poetry is more philosophical than history —that art is a mode of knowledge superior even to science. But Dewey makes an even more extravagant claim, as the following argument shows: he first attacks the representative and cognitive theories, like the play and illusion theories, because all these "isolate one strand in the total experience, a strand that is what it is because of the entire pattern to which it contributes and in which it is absorbed. They take it to be the whole."[53] This statement seems to mean that art is at least what these other theorists claim and more too. Like a number of other theorists, Dewey wants an all-inclusive (eclectic) theory, the most Romantic one of all. Dewey then refers to "a quality of an intense esthetic experience that is so immediate as to be ineffable and mystical," but that is, nevertheless, "the impregnation of sensuous material with imaginative values. . . ."[54] He thinks Plato was guilty of "intellectual ingratitude" because "The forms or Ideas which Plato thought were models and patterns of existing things actually had their source in Greek art. . . ."[55] He concludes this portion of his total argument as follows: "In art as an experience, actuality and possibility or ideality, the new and the old, objective material and personal response, the individual and the universal, surface and depth, sense and meaning, are integrated in an experience in which they are all transfigured from the significance that belongs to them when isolated in reflection. . . . The significance of art as experience is, therefore, incomparable for the adventure of philosophic thought."[56]

To describe the power of art, words like "incomparable" and "transfigured" in the above paragraph join "marvelous aids," "infinitely greater happiness," "transformation" of emotion (which in the last chapter becomes transformation of society), "power to disclose many ideals, a power more germinal and more significant than any revealed ideal, since it includes them in its stride, shatters and remakes them." Through the influence of art, which is "more moral than moralities," "barriers are dissolved, limiting prejudices melt away"; and art results in "common surrender, loyalty and inspiration," as well as in "wide and large redirections of desire and purpose." This list of superlatives found throughout *Art as Experience* make it Dewey's most Romantic book; and it is less guarded in its straining for effect than even his most specifically religious book, *A Common Faith*.

In his chapter "Criticism and Perception," Dewey designates with skill the qualities desirable in criticism of works of art. He describes the weakness of legalistic and judicial criticism—"its inability to cope with the emergence of new modes of life—of experiences that demand new modes of expression."[57] He also objects to the subjectivity of impressionist criticism. Criticism, he says, "is judgment; like every judgment it involves a venture, a hypothetical element; it is directed to qualities which are nevertheless qualities of an *object*; and it is concerned with an individual object, not with making comparisons by means of an external preestablished rule between different things. . . ."[58] "Judgments have a common form because they all have certain functions to perform. These functions are discrimination and unification. Judgment has to evoke a clearer consciousness of constituent parts and to discover how consistently these parts are related to form a whole."[59]

Nothing in this chapter has not been said many times by other writers on esthetics such as H. D. Aiken, Stephen Pepper, Dewitt

Parker, and John Hospers; but Dewey gives fresh expression to these common-sense ideas about the function of criticism. He attacks the reductive fallacy which "exists when some constituent of the work of art is isolated and then the whole is reduced to terms of this single isolated element."[60] As examples of this fallacy, he justly condemns much psychoanalytic and much sociological criticism. He also attacks what he calls a confusion of categories, in which there is an "attempt to translate the distinctively esthetic over into terms of some other kind of experience."[61] Dewey condemns the confusion of esthetic with religious values and says correctly that for esthetic value "the medium and effect are the important matters."[62]

This statement is certainly true, but Dewey seems himself confused when he says in the next sentence, "For this reason, later works of art that have no religious content have a profoundly religious effect."[63] Surely he here should have said "esthetic" rather than "religious," as would seem to be indicated by his explanation in the next sentence: "I imagine the majestic art of 'Paradise Lost' will be more, not less, admitted, and the poem be more widely read, when rejection of its theses of Protestant theology has passed into indifference and forgetfulness."[64] Dewey condemns the confusion of esthetic with philosophic values, and he mentions critical statements by T. S. Eliot and Santayana as examples of such confusion. He certainly oversimplifies T. S. Eliot's criticism when he calls it "fundamentally a moral recipe" on the basis of the following statement by Eliot: "The truest philosophy is the best material for the greatest poet." This statement by Eliot certainly does not, as Dewey says it does, mean "that if we approve the philosophy of Dante we must condemn the poetry of Milton. . . ."[65] Eliot at one time did find fault with the poetry of Milton, but his judgment was based on esthetic considerations; he disapproved of what he considered to be the lack of variety in Milton's lofty rhetoric and its excessive concentration on "the auditory imagination at the expense of the visual and tactile. . . ."[66]

Dewey objects to Santayana's judgment that Shakespeare's poetry is inferior to that of Dante and Homer because, in Shakespeare's philosophy, according to Santayana, "There is no fixed conception of any forces, natural or moral, dominating and transcending our mortal energies." Dewey agrees with Santayana that Shakespeare's philosophy did not include the transcendent, but not with Santayana's further judgment that Shakespeare had no system. Dewey maintains that Shakespeare believed, much like Dewey, in "the free and varied system of nature itself as that works and moves in experience in many and diverse organizations of value."[67] The point to be made here is not to argue whether or not Shakespeare's philosophy was indeed like Dewey's (it may have been) but to note that Dewey, contrary to his own recent admonition, is judging Shakespeare by Shakespeare's philosophy which in Dewey's opinion had "a wholeness and sanity absent from a philosophy of enclosure, transcendence, and fixity."[68]

"The value of experience," says Dewey in elaborating this point, "is not only in the ideals it reveals, but in its power to disclose many ideals, a power more germinal and more significant than any revealed ideal, since it includes them in its stride, shatters and remakes them. One may even reverse the statement and say the value of ideals lies in the experience to which they lead."[69] This statement is like the one (repeated many times in *Logic: The Theory of Inquiry*) that nonexistential generalizations are to be used in connection with observational data to reach an end-in-view. Dewey might here seem to be allowing for the transcendent, but for him ideals are imaginative projections of man himself with no objective referent. As he says concerning Plato's Ideas, Plato should have recognized that these were inspired by (indeed, originated in) human art instead of in some noumenal realm which Plato thought to be real.

Dewey seems in this instance to be putting primary emphasis on the human, but we must remember that in various places elsewhere nature seems to be the leader. For example, we cite once more the following statement: "The striving of man for objects of imagination is a continuation of natural processes; it is something man has learned from the world in which he occurs, not something which he arbitrarily injects into that world. When he adds perception and ideas to these endeavors, it is not after all he who adds; the addition is again the doing of nature and a further complication of its own domain."[70]

Perhaps the explanation of Dewey's ambivalent attitude toward the supremacy of man or nature in evolution may be found in his experience with Hegel. Although he had long ago renounced the philosophy of Hegel (in part because of its ascribing unity to the transcendent World Spirit), still the Hegelian influence, although in a kind of naturalized form, lingers on as experience, which, as Dewey says (see Note 69 above), "discloses many ideals" but then "shatters and remakes them," so that they are "more significant than any revealed ideal." Such a paradoxical synthesis appears again on the same page with Dewey's long quotation from Browning's essay on Shelley, the climax of which is the "imperative call" for a poet who will make a new synthesis that will have an "affinity to something higher—when the positive yet conflicting facts shall again precipitate themselves under a harmonizing law. . . ."[71]

VI Art "More Moral than Moralities . . ."

The climax of *Art as Experience* comes in the final chapter entitled "Art and Civilization," in which art, potentially at least, is said to transform civilization for immense good. For example, "Barriers are dissolved, limiting prejudices melt away, when we enter into the spirit of Negro or Polynesian art. This insensible melting is far more efficacious than the change effected by reasoning, because it enters directly into attitude."[72] Again we have an example of what we have called Dewey's Romantic theorizing. Most critics have stressed Dewey's emphasis on the practical, but the truth is that he is a starry-eyed idealist who admits that his system has not worked in the past but who says that "there is no inherent theoretical bar on my view to some day succeeding." He is answering Reichenbach's objections to his view that "affective [emotional] qualities are products of the doings of nature—of the interaction of an organism and environmental conditions"[73] and are therefore objectively valid; but it is clear that Dewey is hedging, and it appears that he must hedge in the same way concerning his whole system.

For example, an appreciation of Negro or Polynesian art can be no more than an esthetic reaction—a point which Dewey was making throughout most of the chapter preceding this one until he finally was led (by the supposed similarity between his philosophy and Shakespeare's) into claiming more for art than even the best of it can warrant. The same extravagant claim for art is developed throughout this final chapter: "The power of music in particular to merge different individualities in a common surrender, loyalty and inspiration, a power utilized in religion and warfare alike, testifies to the relative universality of the language of art."[74] This statement would be acceptable but for the extravagant moral claims made in "common surrender, loyalty and inspiration."

If art, which is "more moral than moralities,"[75] is the messiah of Dewey's new religion of experience and nature, then, as might be expected, science is his John the Baptist, the voice crying in the wilderness: "The fact that science tends to show that man is part of nature has an effect that is favorable rather than unfavorable to art when its intrinsic significance is realized and when its meaning is no longer interpreted by contrast with beliefs that come to us from the past."[76] Again we are reminded of Shelley's finding religion, which he considered to be a superstition, the main hindrance to progress. Indeed, as we have noted before, Shelley is actually quoted several times in this book, most extensively in this concluding chapter.

After long quotations from both Keats and Shelley, Dewey, who is quite as Romantic in theory as they, concludes thus about the marvelous transforming power of art—if civilization can wait until that distant future when the scientific attitude will become "instinctive—sensuous and immediate, poetic":

> While perception of the union of the possible with the actual in a work of art is itself a great good, the good does not terminate with the immediate and particular occasion in which it is had. The union that is presented in perception persists in the remaking of impulsion and thought. The first intimations of wide and large redirections of desire and purpose are of necessity imaginative. Art is a mode of prediction not found in charts and statistics, and it insinuates possibilities of human relations not to be found in rule and precept, admonition and administration.[77]

In this book, as we have seen, art is the *summum bonum*—"the complete culmination of nature. . . ." Science is subordinated to art as a "handmaiden that conducts events to this happy issue."[78] In spite of Dewey's emphasis on experimental empiricism, however, he never succeeds in convincing us that science will conduct events to this happy issue, in which reasonings may become spontaneous, "instinctive—sensuous and immediate, poetic." How, indeed, does such spontaneity jibe with experimental empiricism or instrumentalism? This transformation, even as a prophetic prospect, is still far from clear when he says that "We have to see science as things will be when the experimental attitude is thoroughly naturalized."[79]

Will we experiment "spontaneously" and come to an "immediate, poetic" conclusion? It certainly takes as much faith to believe this statement as to believe in Isaiah's prophecy that the lion will lie down with the lamb. It is evident that Dewey is a man of great faith and that his faith has logical difficulties quite as great as those of the Judaeo-Christian theology.

CHAPTER 7

Romanticism and Experimental Naturalism: *Logic: The Theory of Inquiry*

L OGIC: *The Theory of Inquiry* is based on "the primary postulate of a naturalistic theory of logic." Such a postulate involves also the "postulate of continuity," or evolution, in which rational operations grow out of organic activities without being identical with that from which they emerge. There is an adjustment of means to consequences in the activities of living creatures, even though not directed by deliberate purposes. This continuity excludes the appearance of a totally new outside force as a cause of change either before or after the beginning of the whole process. Behavior of the biological (pre-intellectual) kind prepares the way for intellectual operations. Although logical activities are much more complex than biological, in both types of activity there is an interaction between the organism and the environment, each causing a change in the other. The key to the transformation from the biological to the logical is the gradual development of language in connection with wider cultural forces. Even the theistic Logos is to be interpreted as the purely human hypostatization of language.

Inquiry, which is the way that logic proceeds, "is the controlled or directed transformation of an indeterminate situation into one that is so determinate in its constituent distinctions and relations as to convert the elements of the original situation into a unified whole." Inquiry "anticipates consequences of what will happen when certain operations are executed under and with respect to observed conditions." Such an anticipation can be successful when perceptual and conceptual materials are correlated with each other. The conceptual materials are correlated with each other. The conceptual materials will include, but not overemphasize, what experience up to the present time has shown to be the best methods available for achieving certain results. Successful experimentation, however, must primarily emphasize changes deliberately introduced to test the validity of existing institutions. So far, this scientific method has been successful mainly in the physical or biological sciences; but it could, if tried, work equally well in morals and religion. Such a method combining nonexistential hypotheses or "ends-in-view" with existential data to reach a satisfactory and ordered solution can work also in the social sciences. Such a scientific approach would remove the prejudice of special-interest groups in social inquiry. In other words, such an approach universally applied would have "enormous cultural consequences" for good.

I *Continuous Development from Biological to Logical*

If we interpret the word *metaphysical* to imply consideration of ultimate origins, then from the very beginning of *Logic: The Theory of Inquiry*[1] and at various places throughout this book Dewey gives metaphysical explanations and violates his earlier statement in *The Influence of Darwin on Philosophy* and elsewhere that "Philosophy forswears inquiry after absolute origins and absolute finalities in order to explore specific values and the specific conditions that generate them."[2] He assumes, even when he does not specifically state, that logic in all its phases had its ultimate origin in Nature with no power beyond or superior to Nature to start or direct the evolutionary development of logic as the outcome of inquiry: "the rational operations grow out of organic activities without being identical with that from which they emerge. There is an adjustment of means to consequences in the activities of living creatures, even though not directed by deliberate purposes."[3] He does not say that organic activities emerged from the primeval protoplasm or that protoplasm evolved from inanimate matter, but presumably this would be implied by his "postulate of continuity."[4]

If we inquired of Dewey how organic activities and then mind could emerge from the primeval protoplasm, Dewey would (and at different times did) give two different answers. In one place he says that the emergence of mind simply happened like the emergence of winds and tides, which means that Nature, and Nature alone, did it. Or he could answer, as he did in his essay on Darwin, that the problem is "insoluble"; for "Once admit that the sole verifiable or fruitful object of knowledge is the particular set of changes that

generate the object of study together with the consequences that
then flow from it, and no intelligible question can be asked about
what, by assumption, lies outside."[5]

Though Dewey obviously did not so intend it, this statement
could be interpreted to assume that something may lie outside
which might be a transcendent God inaccessible by definition to
verifiable inquiry. Indeed, though Dewey does not mention it, the
Darwin of *The Origin of Species* did assume that there was a transcendent God directing the whole wonderful process of evolution,
as the famous final sentence of the book clearly states.[6] Only the
later Darwin became an agnostic because he found so many waste-
ful and destructive activities along with those that appeared to be
the result of benevolent cosmic design. But, to repeat, Dewey—in
Logic: A Theory of Inquiry and in all of his other works after he
abandoned his early devotion to an idealistic world consciousness
of which nature was the expression—held the theory that nature
is the ultimate origin of all that is.

From one standpoint, then, all of *Logic: The Theory of Inquiry*,
like most of Dewey's philosophy, is special pleading for his "primary postulate of a naturalistic theory of logic."[7] If this postulate is
accepted, his argument is an imposing one. The special pleading is
in the implied impossibility of a force greater than Nature as the
source and self-limited director of this great process. "Continuity,"
he says, "excludes the appearance of a totally new outside force as
a cause of changes,"[8] and he clearly intends to exclude any "outside force" before as well as after the beginning (if there was one)
of the whole process.

Dewey indeed sets himself a difficult task in making his naturalistic theory convincing: "If one denies the supernatural," he says,
"then one has the intellectual responsibility of indicating how the
logical may be connected with the biological in a process of continuous development."[9] Dewey does not realize, however, that his
task is more difficult than this, since we can, like Teilhard de Chardin, believe that "the logical may be connected with the biological
in a process of continuous development" and at the same time make
a strong case for a transcendent God, who started and is still directing this process, but who allows mankind (as the culmination at the
present stage of this creation through evolution) freedom to choose
good or evil. Perhaps, as Sidney Hook says,[10] the burden of proof
is on the person who argues for a transcendent God; but certainly

(as Hook should have understood) there is a kind of indirect proof for such a God in the deficiency of Dewey's argument for the naturalistic "postulate." Dewey himself must have recognized that his argument was not completely convincing, for he prefaced his explanation of continuity by saying: "if the following discussion fails to fulfill the task of pointing out satisfactorily the continuous path, then that failure becomes, for those who accept the naturalistic postulate, but a challenge to perform the task better."[11]

Let us see, then, how well Dewey performs his task. He makes it seem easy until we examine closely his explanation of evolution that excludes a transcendent God either before or after the beginning of the whole process. "Intellectual operations," he says, "are foreshadowed in behavior of the biological kind, and the latter prepares the way for the former."[12] The similarity lies in the fact that in both biological and logical activities there is an interaction between the organism and the environment, each causing a change in the other. He does realize that "extraordinary differences . . . mark off the activities and achievement of human beings from those of other biological forms." These differences, he says, "have led to the idea that man is completely separated from other animals by properties that come from a non-natural source."[13]

Again we must keep clearly in mind the position from which he is arguing. There is no question here (and the same is true throughout much of *Logic*) of making a scientific statement which can be verified. He is speculating about origins or an origin; and, in spite of his insistence in his autobiographical essay that he had abandoned absolutism, he remains here an absolutist with nature as his absolute.[14] He insists at times that he is concerned only with continuity, but always implicit (and occasionally, in spite of his caution, explicit) is the idea that the establishment of the principle of continuity disproves a source beyond nature for this whole process. This idea is clearly implicit when, as in the last sentence quoted above, he says that the "extraordinary differences" between human beings and other biological forms have led to the "idea that man is completely separated from other animals by properties that come from a non-natural source." He might seem to be arguing here only against the relatively sudden insertion from a transcendent source into the evolving process of something like "Reason, Intuition and the *A priori*" which would make the transition from the subhuman to the human a "discontinuous" process. We must remember, however, that he leaves no doubt about his position in the initial dependent clause of the following sentence: "If one denies the supernatural, then one has the intellectual responsibility of indicating how the logical may be connected with the biological in a process of continuous development."[15]

In Dewey's opinion the appearance of language enables him to fulfill this responsibility: "development of language (in its widest sense) out of prior biological activities is, in its connection with wider cultural forces, the key to"[16] the transformation from the biological to the logical. His explanation of the gradual development, first, from natural signs (pointing immediately to existential things) to "artificial signs" or word symbols to represent something not existentially present is convincing; but, like Cassirer and Cassirer's American disciple, Mrs. Langer, Dewey overstresses language when he refers to its "power to generate reasoning."[17] In one way, of course, this statement is obviously true, since there cannot be ordered discourse without language; but language can be no more than a tool, as is clear from the existence of nonsense language. Incipient language in various kinds of sounds no doubt preceded reasoning, but the development of language into a tool for reasoning had to be generated by the intelligence that first decided and then remembered that a word should represent (1) a physical object present; (2) gradually a physical object absent; and (3), finally, an abstract idea. The "new dimension" made possible by the use of language as a tool could not have been generated by language but only by the mind that used the language in all its stages.

Even if it may seem that this argument about the temporal priority of language or mind is like that over the priority of the chicken or egg (and that we have merely taken the opposite side from Dewey), it still remains true that Dewey has not successfully made his point that the development of language is "the key to" (in the sense of adequately explaining) the continuity between the biological and the logical. At least William James (whose emphasis in his most important book, *Principles of Psychology*, on the biological origins of psychology greatly influenced Dewey's argument) is far from finding the transition from the pre-mental to the mental as easily explained as Dewey attempts to explain it. James can only conclude in the final sentence of the *Principles* that "the more sincerely one seeks to trace the actual course of *psychogenesis*, the steps by which as a race we may have come by the peculiar mental attributes which we possess, the more clearly one perceives 'the slowly gathering twilight close in utter night.' "[18]

And (to mention only one other example among many that could be cited from eminent thinkers of this century) René Dubos, one of the world's foremost microbiologists and experimental pathologists, said in 1962: "But what first made *Homo sapiens* develop self-consciousness, plan for the future, and thus become qualitatively different from the rest of creation, is as mysterious as ever."[19] Dubos also quotes with approval the following statement by MacDonald Critchely about the development of language: "Even in the case of the most untutored, primitive savage human communities, the language system is so far removed in its complexity from the crude and simple utterances of the sagest of the primates, as to be scarcely comparable. And nowhere and at no time has there been any hint of an approximation between these two extremes. Can it be, therefore, that a veritable rubicon does exist between animals and men after all?"[20]

All Dewey's argument about language is, of course, part of the task of connecting the logical and the biological which he feels that one "who denies the supernatural" must assume. A further part of this task, in his opinion, is to interpret the theistic *Logos* as the purely human hypostatization of language, "in its syntactical structure and its wealth of meaning contents,"[21] and to condemn the theistic interpretation for having "held back for centuries the development of inquiries of a kind that are competent to deal with the problems of the existent world."[22]

II *The Argument of Teilhard de Chardin*

To repeat, Dewey has a harder task than he realizes; for continuous development from the biological to the logical does not, though he seems to think that it does, disprove a supernatural origin for the whole process. Others before Pierre Teilhard de Chardin have argued for a gradual evolution of the life process begun and (within limits) guided by one all-wise and all-powerful God, but Chardin's *The Phenomenon of Man*[23] seems to be the most impressive argument of this kind that has yet appeared. Since Chardin was a very distinguished paleontologist, his metaphysical speculations were carefully based on the most expert scientific study and have commanded much attention and respect. Chardin goes far beyond Dewey in stressing the principle of continuity. "To make room for thought

100

in the world," says Chardin, "I have needed to 'interiorise' matter,"[24] and this "Without" and "Within"[25] he has proceeded to posit in the most primitive matter, the "Within" being a most rudimentary kind of "psychicism," from which in due time full consciousness was to emerge. He is happy to find his idea of "pre-life" supported by the eminent biologist J. B. S. Haldane, from whom he quotes the following: "We do not find obvious evidence of life or mind in so-called inert matter, and we naturally study them most easily where they are most completely manifested; but if the scientific point of view is correct, we shall ultimately find them, at least in rudimentary forms, all through the universe."[26]

Much of Chardin's interpretation of evolution is also supported by another distinguished naturalist, Sir Julian Huxley, who refers to the "positive value of Chardin's naturalistic general approach." Huxley, of course, finds it "impossible to follow Chardin all the way in his gallant attempt to reconcile the supernatural elements in Christianity with the facts and implications of evolution,"[27] but he offers no arguments beyond this mild statement of disagreement. Dewey would probably have interpreted this statement as only a "gallant" refusal by Huxley to demolish Chardin's connection of a "naturalistic" approach to evolution with the belief in a transcendent God, but Huxley's further comments along this point indicate that he does indeed follow the metaphysical part of Chardin's argument further than the naturalistic postulate would seem to allow: "the concept of a hyperpersonal mode or organization," says Huxley, "sprang [and the implication is that it might logically spring] from Père Teilhard's conviction of the supreme importance of personality. . . . This belief in the pre-eminent was for him a matter of faith, but of faith supported by rational enquiry and scientific knowledge. It prevented him from diluting his concept of the divine principle inherent in reality, in a vague and meaningless pantheism, just as his apprehension of the entire process of reality as a system of interrelations, and of mankind as actively participating in that process, saved him from losing his way in the deserts of individualism and existentialism."[28]

Huxley also expresses agreement with Chardin's belief that the further progress of evolution meant "The incipient development of mankind into a single psychosocial unit, with a single noosystem or common pool of thought. . . . It remains for our descendants to organise this global noosystem more adequately, so as to enable mankind to understand the process of evolution on earth more fully and to direct it more adequately."[29] Huxley, who fully agrees with this statement, adds: "I had independently expressed something of the same sort, by saying that in modern scientific man, evolution was at last becoming conscious of itself—a phrase which I found delighted Père Teilhard. His formulation, however, is more profound and more seminal: it implies that we should consider interthinking humanity as a new type of organism, whose destiny it is to realize new possibilities for evolving life on this planet."[30]

Huxley may not have known exactly why his statement that evolution was at last becoming conscious of itself delighted Chardin; it was probably because Chardin realized that, for most people, the naturalistic position would be an insufficient foundation for this cosmically optimistic prospect for mankind. Only with the assistance of a transcendent God, toward whom as the "Omega Point" in this cosmic process mankind is painfully and slowly struggling, can the distant goal be reached. Indeed, without such assistance, how could evolution, beginning with the most primitive matter (which must have been "interiorised" even at that stage) have become "conscious of itself"? At least, such an argument is quite as convincing as Dewey's substitution of nature for the transcendent God.

Furthermore, Dewey's assertion that the universe is now (by contrast with the prevailing thought in Classical Greece) "conceived of as open and in process"[31] fits perfectly the pattern of growth as described by Chardin. Dewey seems to think that every argument which emphasizes process, continuity, and openness helps to confirm his postulate of a purely naturalistic logic. But this process of human and cosmic growth applies to Chardin's biblical interpretation of the agonizing process of evolution as, in Saint Paul's words, "the whole creation groaning and travailing" in its struggle upward toward the "Omega Point," which lies far in the future but toward which great progress has already been made. This whole process of continuing creation, according to Chardin, is under the divine guidance of the "cosmic Christ" but is at the same time paradoxically consistent with man's freedom. Dewey believes in man's freedom in his struggle upward but acknowledges assistance from no force greater than Nature (sometimes lower case n), between which and man there is a constant collaboration. In fact, Dewey considers belief in a transcendent God to be actually an obstacle to true progress.

Critics such as Robert J. Roth, however, think that Dewey was closer to Christianity than he knew, that "his thought, like every-thing else, was in 'process,' growing, developing . . . even saying, more than was explicitly intended."[32] Some, such as George R. Geiger,[33] have even made of Dewey a theist in spite of himself. It seems more accurate to say that Dewey was at times, with his "natural piety," a kind of pantheist. (Dewey, as we have seen, referred to his religious attitude as "like the poetic pantheism of Wordsworth and Walt Whitman's sense of oneness with the universe.")[34] But to treasure Dewey's attitude toward religion as a support for believers in a transcendent God is, it would seem, dangerously like harboring a Trojan horse. Roth finds inspiration in the "indefinite, tentative, probing" thought of Dewey because, he says, "Dewey has not effectively eliminated a directive force in nature. Objectively his thought is open to any extension which may be made of thrust, even, one might add, to an extension to a tran-scendantal. Dewey would say, of course, that such an extension is impossible. But, at least in his analysis of ends, he has not demon-strated this impossibility."[35]

This argument, it would seem, gives Dewey a great deal more credit spiritually than he deserves. Of course, Dewey has not "eliminated a directive force in nature"; he did not try to. Instead, he substituted Nature for the transcendent World Spirit in which, following Hegel, he believed during his early days. Nature, to be sure, is probably just as good a guide as Hegel's absolute con-sciousness, of which everything that happens, good or bad, is an expression and through which all is for the unified best. Indeed, in Dewey's *Art as Experience*, he seems—in his exaltation of the great rhythms of life (including even its catastrophes)—almost to be returning to his early mentor. But neither Nature nor Hegel's World Spirit is an effective substitute or support for the transcendent God of Christianity. We might as well make an "extension of the thrust" of Comte's Humanity-God or any of the pagan gods. Roth is, some-what too graciously, looking from the standpoint of his own belief in an all-wise, benevolent transcendent God to Dewey's "directive force in nature" and wishing to give credit to Dewey's "social awareness" and "notion of community."

III   *Humanization of the Divine Through Logic as Inquiry*

If Dewey's intermittent and mitigated pantheism applied to

evolution appears in this book, so also does another aspect of his philosophy of religion: the concept of divinity as an eventual function arising in and useful for inquiry. Dewey can only imply some such reduction of the idea of God and/or exaltation of man as this when he translates the Platonic doctrine of the One and the Many into the terms of his own logic. "Unity, or The One," he says, "is the existential counterpart of the product of operations which, by institution of agreement of different contents in evidential force, establish warranted identities. Negation, on the other hand, discriminates and produces differences. The latter when hypostatized constitute the Many. . . . The insoluble problems which have led to speculative metaphysical constructions about the One and the Many arise from making entities, expressed in nouns, out of processes and operations properly designated by active verbs and adverbs."[36] Elsewhere, Dewey has sanctioned the use of the term "God" when it refers to the conscious projection of man's ideals as a part of the means to be used in inquiry. Here likewise the One (or God) is really a part (but a completely human part) of "processes and operations properly designated by active verbs and adverbs."

It is, then, no wonder that Dewey found Emerson such a congenial spirit—that is, that part of Emerson whose transcendental God was really only man himself in self-inspired action. Indeed, the early Hegelian Dewey could accept and admire the Emersonian Over-Soul, even when it meant, as sometimes it did for Emerson, more than man and nature; but we have already noticed Dewey's abrupt, even violent, rejection of any power greater than Nature early in his career.

IV *Knowledge Used to Produce Enjoyment and Relieve Suffering*

In Chapter IV, "Common Sense and Scientific Inquiry," Dewey again gives his definition of knowledge as directly related to practical consequences. An object, he says, "is noted or 'known' only so far as guidance is thereby given to direction of behavior; so that the situation in which it is found can be appropriately enjoyed or some of its conditions be so used that enjoyment will result or suffering be obviated."[37] If this statement makes him sound like a hedonist (however refined), we must realize that is not his intent; but his statement once more calls attention to the dangers of his making consequences the ultimate criterion for determining procedure.

Consequences are to be determined by each individual; and, in the field of personal morals (where Dewey thinks that this pragmatic test is especially needed), it is almost inevitable that one of low morals who approaches a moral problem will not, for several reasons, be led to elevate his standards by observing the consequences of his deeds: (1) In many cases the hedonistic consequences of low moral standards will seem to be highly satisfactory—wealth, material success, fame (at least notoriety), etc.; this satisfaction will of course involve a certain amount of rationalization, but even the best of humans all too often rationalize in defense of their actions. (2) Even if one recognizes the evil of his ways and sincerely wishes to improve, he may well lack the will power to attain or maintain improved standards. To mention extreme cases (but ones very numerous in our civilization), narcotics addicts usually regret the crimes which they commit to maintain their habit. (Of course, it could be argued that such problems involve disease rather than morality; but, despite all our artificial assistance toward cures, only the victim's exertion of will, which means moral effort, can complete the cure.) These examples illustrate the inadequacy of Dewey's making consequences the ultimate guide even if the individual fully recognizes that the consequences of his past deeds are bad.

Of course, Dewey admits, as we have noted, that his system has not yet been applied to morals and religion; and he thinks that this failure explains why so much is wrong in these areas—so little progress, in his opinion, as compared with that made in the realm of material welfare. He can see no good reason why his method has not been applied because, in his opinion, it is simply *the* method of intelligence, and who could logically be opposed to the use of intelligence rather than ignorance? What Dewey cannot realize is that his pragmatic naturalism is not, after all, the only method of intelligence. There are indeed intelligent arguments for belief in a transcendent God. To mention only one among many, we quote from Kant: "it is absolutely impossible for us to produce from nature itself grounds of explanation for purposive combinations; and it is necessary by the constitution of the human cognitive faculties to seek the supreme ground of these purposive combinations in an original Understanding as the cause of the world."[38] The theist may also argue intelligently that the most careful inquiry (one that would satisfy Dewey's rigorous demands) in morals has indicated that the ethical conduct of most people is most effectively improved when (along with the exertion of will referred to above) they consider themselves to be obeying the commands of a Supreme and Benevolent Being.

For example, drunkards and narcotics addicts have in the past been, and are now being, reformed or (if we will) cured. How many of these have been reformed (or cured) by merely applying Dewey's method of observing the consequences of their actions? If the testimony of organizations like Alcoholics Anonymous is to be admitted, all of those reformed have depended in part on some kind of divine (as well as human) assistance along with the utmost exertion of their own will power. Dewey might insist that such dependence was superfluous and even illusory, but he could only speculate here, and the empirical evidence would seem to be against him.[39] Dewey again and again regrets that the scientific method of testing by consequences has had little effect "In the region of highest importance to common sense, namely, that of moral, political, economic ideas and beliefs, and the methods of forming and confirming them. . . ."[40] On the contrary, it might well be argued that the present chaos in morals is, at least in part, due to the application in the past and present of the principle of testing by consequences. The curse of America, as William James said (although he himself was a devoted pragmatist), is "The moral flabbiness born of the exclusive worship of that bitch-goddess success,"[41] and what is such worship but a dependence for guidance on consequences?

There is, then, grave danger of the intrusion of hedonism in Dewey's emphasis on consequences (to be evaluated by personal satisfaction), and he does not remove these dangers[42] even when he warns that "It is not bare enjoyment but enjoyments as consummation of previous processes and responses that constitutes appreciation,"[43] for hedonism is capable of great refinement—as may be seen, for example, in the works of Pater, whose esthetic interpretation of the religion of the Middle Ages is accepted by Dewey. In fact, as we have seen before, there is at times in Dewey himself, unyielding moral activist though he usually is, an element of hedonism. "The history of man," as he says apparently with approval in *Experience and Nature*, "shows that man takes his enjoyment neat, and at short range as possible."[44] Of course, as we noted earlier, Dewey is trying to be both moderately Dionysian and completely Apollonian at the same time; and such an attempted combination of opposites is no doubt the result of his early admiration for Hegel, which, as he said, "left a permanent deposit" in his thinking.

Another example of this attempt to combine the Romantic and the Classical is expressed in the following sentence, which may be said to contain the theme of *Art as Experience*, and it is similar to the implications of his logic in *Logic: The Theory of Inquiry*: "Art is the living and concrete proof that man is capable of restoring consciously, and thus on the plane of meaning, the union of sense, need, impulse, and action characteristic of the live creature."[45] As Professor Melvin Rader has said in a similar vein, "Art is the great reconciler of opposite poles which, in our practical life, ordinarily exclude each other. More than any other form of human experience, it combines such contrasting moments as variety and unity, familiarity and strangeness, repose and stimulation, order and spontaneity, the Apollonian and the Dionysian moods."[46]

Dewey, however, is even more Hegelian or Romantic[47] than Professor Rader; for Dewey these opposite poles (eventually) need not "ordinarily exclude each other" even "in our practical life." Such, as we have seen, is the faith of the great Romantic, who supposedly bases his predictions only on a thoroughly adequate amount of scientific evidence. He admits that so far he has very little evidence that the scientific techniques so successful in improving our material welfare can be successfully used in transforming our morals, but he insisted with prophetic fervor to the very end that "there is no inherent theoretical bar on my view to some day succeeding."[48]

V   *Nonexistential Hypotheses and Existential Data Combined*

The rest of Dewey's *Logic*, like the whole massive book, is an excellent statement of logical procedures which have been most successful in transforming our material welfare. He shows, for example, that even the "purest" mathematics almost always becomes eventually applicable to physical existence. Indeed, he says, "That the range of existential applicability of mathematical subject-matter is in direct ratio to its abstractness is shown by the history of physical science in its relation to the history of mathematical science."[49] Because of the complexity of the operations, a new set of symbols constituting a new technical language is often needed.

Nonexistential hypotheses and existential data derived from physical observation are combined to reach "a coherent individualized situation."[50] Once more Dewey warns, as he has warned many times before, against the Aristotelian belief that "general propositions represent a direct notation of an inherent static structure, or essence. . . ."[51] "Unless conceptual subject-matter is interpreted solely and wholly on the ground of the function it performs in the conduct of inquiry, this difficulty in dimensions between the conceptual and the existential creates a basic philosophic problem."[52]

All this argument, though by no means new, is freshly and cogently stated—cogently, that is, until Dewey attempts in Chapter XXIV to transfer his argument in all its details from the physical to the social sciences. There are, to be sure, certain obvious similarities; and Dewey carefully explores these. He notes that most analyses of social ills are based on prejudiced opinions without sufficient evidence. Of course, such prejudice exists, almost always on both sides in social conflicts; but the main problem for Dewey is the construction of an end-in-view or an hypothesis by scientific means. "Hypotheses," he says, "have to be formed and tested in strict correlativity with existential conditions as means. . . ."[53]

Dewey apparently thinks that the scientific approach would remove the prejudice of special interest groups in social inquiry. In other words, this "working hypothesis or experimental method applies to the facts which it concerns and effects a better ordering." Dewey says[54] that this statement of Dominique Parodi, one of his devoted followers, proves that "long before the *Logic* was written some readers were able to derive from what I wrote a correct idea." Supposedly "a better ordering" guarantees that the satisfaction pragmatically attained is not "merely a means for a practical end."[55] But "a better ordering" need not be a moral ordering, and the sad fact remains that special interest groups often approach the attainment of their "ends-in-view" with all the scientific precision, including assessment of consequences, that Dewey and his followers think would eliminate such bias. Inquiry, as Dewey says, may be a self-corrective process; but the correction may be a technical one aimed at the aggrandizement of an individual or the members of a selfish group.

Of social enterprises Dewey says, "Without systematic formulation of ruling ideas, inquiry is kept in the domain of opinion and action in the realm of conflict."[56] This statement seems to mean that with such a formulation conflict would be avoided—surely a naïve and unwarranted dependence on the scientific approach. The Communists, for example, have been completely scientific in their approach to the problem of class conflict; they have combined nonexistential hypotheses with existential observed data to get unified wholes (rigid control) in every country which they now dominate. More specifically, to use another of Dewey's key statements about correct logical procedure, we can be sure that, for the Communist party, "in logical fact, perceptual and conceptual materials are instituted in functional correlativity with each other . . . and are finally checked by their capacity to introduce a resolved unified situation."[57] Furthermore, after "effecting a better ordering" and a "unified whole," the Communists with great care have used "the conclusions of a given inquiry" as a "means of carrying on further inquiries."[58]

In fact, Dewey himself was for a time in the 1920's convinced that much good was being accomplished in the Soviet Union. As his daughter Miss Jane Dewey tells us, "His [Dewey's] membership in a visiting group of American educators brought him into relations with remarkable Russian men and women, teachers and students, who were ardently convinced of the necessary place of education with a social aim and cooperative methods in making secure the purposes of the revolution. . . . The impression he derived from these associations was so unlike the beliefs current in the United States that he wrote a series of articles very sympathetic in tone with the U.S.S.R., which led to his being described as a 'Bolshevik' and a 'red' in the conservative press."[59]

Of course, Dewey, like various other high-minded observers, changed his mind in the light of additional evidence because he was not then "satisfied" with what he saw; but the Communists were satisfied, and their opinion was formed from observing the same consequences. To repeat, a "better ordering" need not be a more moral ordering; and on this fundamental ambiguity Dewey's theory of inquiry breaks down.

Hook may be correct in saying that "Dewey's logical theory is the most ambitious attempt ever made to formulate the rationale of modern scientific method."[60] Its ambitiousness, however, lies mainly in Dewey's claim, admittedly as yet unsubstantiated, that it is as applicable to any other realm—for example, that of personal or social morality—as it has been to the production of all the material objects that made and have followed the Industrial Revolution. Hook is perfectly satisfied with Dewey's answer to those who question him about the source of standards in his logical theory. "Dewey's answer," says Hook with approval, "is that they are selectively derived from the continuum of inquiries; and that they function regulatively whenever they are explicitly set up as a guide to subsequent inquiry."[61] It is just that simple; and, if we find it too simple, Hook, perhaps the leading contemporary disciple of Dewey, tells us that what Dewey discovered about the reason why "certain standards are set up rather than others to regulate and to test ongoing inquiries" was "originally found in Peirce"[62]; and we must indeed be rather dense, so the implication is, if we are not then satisfied.

The explanation, supposedly fortified by Peirce,[63] is that "Human beings make inferences as naturally, even if not so frequently, as they eat, drink, and make merry."[64] Certain inferences, as Dewey says, "yield conclusions that are stable and productive in further inquiries"[65]; others do not. So, just as naturally as we eat, drink, and make merry, we form our standards from the first type of inquiries; and they then become "normative and necessary" and "binding"[66] on our future conduct. The main obstacle for Dewey to the establishment of this scientifically based millennium is the stultifying and superstitious belief in eternal principles (or some vaguely personalized variant thereof like a transcendent God). Perhaps in Nature's good time we shall learn to remove this obstacle "as naturally as we eat, drink, and make merry"; and, having done so, we will have the occasion to make even merrier—for we shall be well along on the Deweyan road to "instituting a logic based inclusively and exclusively upon the operations of inquiry," and this will have "enormous cultural consequences."[67]

Such is the faith of the great Romanticist in the easy applicability of the scientific method to morals, but such argument is not likely to convince those who take a more realistic view of human nature.

CHAPTER 8

Dewey and His Contemporaries

I *Dewey and William James: Similarities and Differences*

T HE two contemporaries of Dewey to whom he was most indebted were Charles Sanders Peirce and William James, and most of Dewey's views were quite similar to those of the school of logical empiricists—Rudolf Carnap, Charles W. Morris, and others —although he sharply condemned this group for reasons that seem hard to explain. In spite of the fact that Dewey was indebted to James's *Principles of Psychology* for his emphasis on the continuity between the biological and the logical, his own brand of pragmatism differed from that of James, as Dewey explained in his review of James's *Pragmatism*. For example, Dewey says that James at times seemed to maintain that

> . . . any good which flows from acceptance of a belief is treated as if it were an evidence, *in so far*, of the truth of the idea. This holds particularly when theological notions are under consideration. . . . Since Mr. James has referred to me as saying, "truth is what gives satisfaction," I may remark (apart from the fact that I do not think I ever said that truth is what *gives* satisfaction) that I have never identified any satisfaction with the truth of an idea, save *that* satisfaction which arises when the idea as working hypothesis or tentative. method is applied to prior existences in such a way as to fulfill what it intends.[1]

As regards particularly "theological notions," Dewey wanted it clearly understood that, in his opinion, no satisfaction derived from belief in God could in any way be used as an indication of the existence of God. Dewey's objection was mainly to James's later writings after the *Principles of Psychology*, as the above passage and the following portion of a letter to James indicate: "I find (in conversation) that many critics regard your doctrine as much more subjectivistic than mine, because I, following the lead of your *Psychology*, 'Reflex-Action and Theism' etc., emphasize (more than do your later writings) the biological *origin* of ideas and intellectual operations."[2] Dewey also objected to James's labeling Dewey's universe as "ontological," for this term had connotations of the idealism from which Dewey had broken away. In other words, Dewey wanted it clearly understood that in his view evolution proceeded from the physical to the psycho-physical and then the mental in a continuous development (cf. discussion in Chapter 3 above), and reference to an "ontological" universe might imply that everything had originated in, and was still guided by, a great World-Consciousness, as Hegel had argued. Furthermore, "ontology" might be confused with "ontologism," the belief that the knowledge of God is immediate and intuitive, and that all other knowledge is dependent upon this.

But these criticisms of James seem remarkably mild in view of the great differences between Dewey's naturalistic monism (cf. Chapter 3 above) and James's restless exploration into "a pluralistic universe." We may consider, for example, the following passage from James:

> . . . the only way to escape from the paradoxes and perplexities that a consistently thought-out monistic universe suffers from . . . is to be frankly pluralistic and assume that the superhuman consciousness, however vast it may be, has itself an external environment, and consequently is finite. . . . The analogies with ordinary psychology and with the facts of pathology, with those of psychical research, so called, and with those of religious experience, establish, when taken together, a decidedly *formidable* probability in favor of a general view of the world almost identical with Fechner's . . . with his distinct earth-soul functioning as our guardian angel. . . . Fechner's ideas are not without direct empirical verification.[3]

This "piecemeal supernaturalism" surely must have seemed to Dewey (in his post-Hegelian period at least) to be a wild kind of speculation, second only to the wholesale supernaturalism of religious orthodoxy; but, strangely enough, Dewey seldom mentioned (and even then objected only mildly to) James's "theological notions." As Perry says, both James and Dewey "sought by sympathy and understanding to emphasize the truth which they held in common, rather than by disputation to aggravate their differences."[4]

II *Dewey and the Logical Empiricists*

Dewey's lifelong attitude of admiration for James and for Peirce (to be considered in detail later) is all the more difficult to explain when we note his rather waspish hostility to a group of philosophers, the logical empiricists, whose fundamental position (especially in their attitude toward the metaphysical) was far closer to that of Dewey than were the views of Peirce and James. The logical empiricists considered pragmatism, as Carnap says, "as an ally in their fight against traditional metaphysics"; and Carnap praised the work of Dewey as being "especially prominent" in "investigations concerning the pragmatic component in language."[5] But Dewey was never really friendly to this group and became less so as he grew older; to him, they seemed to be multiplying entities beyond necessity[6] although actually their views, on all but minor points, were very similar to his, as appears from the following comparison.

First, Dewey and the logical empiricists agreed that the scientific method was applicable to and desirable for all phases of life that could profitably be investigated. Traditional metaphysics, of course, as Carnap said, was the common enemy. Carnap admitted that the logical empiricists had concentrated in their early days too exclusively on the foundations of physics and mathematics and had given insufficient attention to clarifying the methods of the social sciences, but he insisted that the theoretical theses of logical empiricism "give support to the view that strictly scientific methods are applicable also to the investigation of men, groups, and societies, and thereby they help to strengthen the attitude which is a precondition for the development of more reasonable forms of the social order."[7] The adherents of logical empiricism have always, he said, "just like Russell, Dewey, and their followers . . . criticized the existing order of society as unreasonable and have demanded that it should be reformed on the basis of scientific insights and careful planning in such a way that the needs and aspirations of all would be satisfied as far as possible; this attitude is the core of our scientific humanism."[8]

Furthermore, says Carnap (and how could one be more like Dewey than this?), "our physicalistic and naturalistic conceptions are diametrically opposed to any dualism that divorces human spirit from natural process, and . . . emphasize that man with all his experience in the various spheres of life, not excluding those of philosophical thinking, is just a part of the one all-embracing nature."[9] Dewey insisted, however, that he was a realist and that the logical positivists or logical empiricists were idealists. Carnap insists that, for the logical empiricists, the controversies about the reality or irreality of the external world, of other minds, and of abstract entities are not theoretically meaningful; "but we can still give them meaning by reinterpreting them or, more exactly, by replacing them with the practical questions concerning the choice of certain language forms."[10]

Seemingly the word *practical* here (in connection with the reform of the existing order of society—"just like Russell, Dewey, and their followers"—demanded by Carnap, as quoted above) indicates that Dewey and Bentley are not justified in accusing Carnap of interpreting "the words man utters as independent beings—logicians' playthings, akin to magicians' vipers or children's fairies. . . ." Certainly Carnap would agree with them that "the man who talks and thinks and knows belongs to the world in which he has been evolved in all his talkings, thinkings and knowings. . . . Not even in his latest and most complex activities is it well to survey this natural man as magically 'emergent' into something new and strange."[11]

Indeed, Carnap argues specifically against *emergentism*, as in the following statement: "As a specific argument against the doctrine of *emergentism* . . . I should like to emphasize in the contest the philosophically important fact that scientific investigations demonstrate ever more clearly a *continuity* in the evolution of man."[12] Carnap is thus saying exactly what Dewey said—that man did not "magically emerge into something new and strange"—that is, radically different from lower forms of life—as the theory of "emergentism" in evolution maintains, but that the development of man from these lower forms was a very gradual and continuous process. Carnap believes, like Dewey, that "all laws of nature, including those which hold for organisms, human beings, and human societies, are logical consequences of the physical laws, i. e., of those laws which are needed for the explanation of inorganic processes."[13]

There is also no essential difference between the pragmatists and the logical empiricists concerning the nature of value judgments. Of course, Carnap is primarily an "emotivist," holding that "true" and "false" (and thus "cognitive meaning") are inapplicable to value judgments; Dewey is a "cognitivist," holding that value judgments may be either true or false and, as Reichenbach said of Dewey's view, "are statements of fact in a sense analogous to statements of physical facts."[14] But Abraham Kaplan (in a brilliant article tracing two decades of controversy between these two theories) has demonstrated that the "emotivist" and "cognitivist" positions are fundamentally alike, with only minor differences. He summarizes the similarities as follows:

> Emotivists and cognitivists alike recognize the importance of cognitive considerations in arriving at judgments of value. The difference is only that, since the former deny cognitive meaning to such judgments, these considerations cannot be admitted by them to provide "reasons" in a logical sense. . . . Emotivists like Stevenson are willing to grant cognitive *function* to emotive meaning, while withholding cognitive content. . . .
>
> The cognitivist focusses attention on the content of the value judgment, the emotivist on its function; the former is interested in the matters of fact entering into this content, the latter in the relation of these matters of fact to desire and volition, which alone gives the facts a value reference. . . .
>
> Whatever differences there are that are not merely matters of emphasis are considerably lessened by the provision in emotivism of devices by which attitudes, and ways of changing them, can be rationally criticized. An emotivism which formulates criteria (like the procedural norms discussed earlier) for the appraisal of attitudes—as impartial or biased, rooted in comprehensive and true beliefs or in incomplete and misleading ones, expressing arbitrary caprice or resulting from careful reflection—such an emotivism is very little different in substance from cognitivism.[15]

In view, then, of all the important similarities between Dewey and the logical positivists, it would have seemed both gracious and reasonable for him to welcome them as allies in the struggle against the metaphysical. Instead, he attacked them frequently and viciously. Typical is the rather blunt advice which he gave C. W. Morris, one of the outstanding logical empiricists: " 'Users' of Peirce's writings should either stick to his basic pattern or leave him alone."[16] Morris, who replied in a polite note, denied that he had attempted either to imitate or to correct Peirce.[17] There is not space here to explore the complex controversy between Dewey and Morris, but the important point is that, in so far as they both considered Peirce as an ally in their rejection of the metaphysical, they were both mistaken. Dewey was, as we shall see, guilty of distorting Peirce's "basic pattern" by carefully isolating the parts of Peirce's philosophy that seem (when taken out of context) to reinforce naturalism, and by ignoring Peirce's very detailed explanation that his whole philosophy of pragmaticism is a reinforcement of the "Neglected Argument" for a transcendent God.

III *Peirce and Dewey: Superficial Similarity and Basic Contrast*

In studying the relation between Peirce and Dewey, the first thing to be noticed is that Dewey's references to Peirce are almost aways complimentary, even though Peirce's complimentary references to Dewey are always sharply qualified. For example, Peirce's letter to Dewey concerning Dewey's contributions to the *Studies in Logical Theory* (1903) contains the following sharp rebuke:

> If then you have a "Natural History" (i.e. a comparative anatomy) of thought,—it is not the merely *possible* thought that Normative Science studies, but thought as it presents itself in an *apparently* inexplicable and irrational experience.
>
> The effect of teaching that such a Natural History can take the place of a normative science of thought must be to render the rules of reasoning lax; and in fact I find you and your students greatly given over to what to me seems like a debauch of loose reasoning.[18]

When Peirce also attacked *Studies in Logical Theory* in a review in *The Nation,* the review[19] was worded more mildly than the letter, presumably because of Peirce's personal regard for Dewey. At any rate, Dewey never attempted to answer Peirce's criticism, but always praised him highly and considered his own philosophy (especially in *Logic: The Theory of Inquiry*) to be an outgrowth of Peirce's. There are some surface similarities between the philosophy of Peirce and that of Dewey, but there is a fundamental difference which is carefully (certainly not carelessly) ignored by Dewey—the fact that Peirce considered his "Scientific Metaphysics," which pointed very positively to a transcendent God, to be an important part of his "Pragmaticism," the name to which he changed his philosophy after his pragmatism had been distorted by most of those who had adopted it.

The editors of *Volume VI* of the *Collected Papers of Peirce* say that "The second book of the volume, devoted to religion or 'psychical metaphysics,' has rather tenuous connections with the rest of the system."[20] Since they do not elaborate, the editors apparently think that this statement will be self-evident to readers of this volume; but the truth is that Peirce has made a strong case from the very first for his contention that his system "is a theory of logical analysis, or true definition; and its merits are greatest in its application to the highest metaphysical conceptions."[21] We do not need to argue, as does Professor John E. Smith,[22] that Peirce's interest in metaphysics and religion is not surprising since a fertile mind like his could be expected to examine a wide variety of subjects, Smith's implication being that there is no vital connection between Peirce's religion and the rest of his pragmaticism.

Peirce contends—and there seems to be no solid argument refuting his contention—that "the N.A. [Neglected Argument] is the First State of a scientific inquiry, resulting in a hypothesis of the very highest plausibility, whose ultimate test must lie in its value in the self-controlled growth of man's conduct of life. . . ."[23] In other words, it is clearly implied in Peirce's most often quoted essay, "How to Make Our Ideas Clear," that even ideas about the existence of a transcendent God can be made clear and forceful enough so that they will be "directly applicable to the conduct of life, and full of nutrition for man's highest growth," but we may not be able to understand all the implications of the argument "as a proposition of metaphysical theology."[24] Indeed, toward the end of this essay he says that "we should not, perhaps, be making a pretension so presumptuous as it would be singular, if we were to offer a metaphysical theory of existence for universal acceptance among those who employ the scientific method of fixing belief."[25]

This approach to "Scientific Metaphysics" bears obvious resemblances to that of Kant, who also claimed to establish a scientific basis for belief in God. If it seems that Peirce emphasizes some kind of knowledge of God in contrast to Kant's controversial statement that knowledge of God is impossible, it must be remembered that Kant later modified his view to allow for a "practical" knowledge of God, freedom, and immortality. Besides this general similarity to Kant (which is all that is claimed), we shall see later that Peirce's interpretation of science as pointing to the metaphysical presages a very noticeable trend among prominent scientists in recent years; but now we must consider further the manner in which Peirce uses science in his approach to God in a way which would have been condemned by Dewey if it had been taken by any other scientist but which in Peirce Dewey neither notices nor condemns.

The following quotation is from Peirce's "Scientific Metaphysics": "If God Really be, and be benign, then, in view of the generally conceded truth that religion, were it but proved, would be a good outweighing all others, we should naturally expect that there would be some Argument for His Reality that should be obvious to all minds, high and low alike, that should earnestly strive to find the truth of the matter; and further, that this Argument should present its conclusion, not as a proposition of metaphysical theology, but in a form directly applicable to the conduct of life, and full of nutrition for man's highest growth."[26] Peirce then proceeds to give in detail the "Neglected Argument," in which "religious meditation" is "allowed to grow spontaneously from Pure Play without any breach of continuity," and in which "psychological speculations will naturally lead on to musings upon metaphysical problems proper . . . certain lines of reflection which will inevitably suggest the hypothesis of God's Reality."[27] Then, under the section entitled "Pragmaticism," referring to a hypothetical thinker, he says:

This brings him, for testing the hypothesis [of God's Reality], to taking his stand upon Pragmaticism, which implies faith in common sense and in instinct, though only as they issue from the cupel-furnace of measured criticism. In short, he will say that the N.A. [Neglected Argument] is the First State of a scientific inquiry, resulting in a hypothesis of the very highest Plausibility, whose ultimate test must lie in its value in the self-controlled growth of man's conduct of life. . . . This, I beg to point out, is a very different position from that of Mr. Schiller and the pragmatists of today. . . . It seems to me a pity that they should allow a philosophy so instinct with life to become infected with seeds of death in such notions as that of the unreality of all ideas of infinity and that of the mutability of truth, and in such confusions of thought as that of active willing (willing to control thought, to doubt, and to weigh reasons) with willing not to exert the will (willing to believe).[28]

We have quoted at length to indicate that Peirce considered as essential to his pragmaticism its metaphysical implications, of which we would hardly be aware if (without reading Peirce) we depended on Dewey's article entitled "The Pragmatism of Peirce," written as a supplementary essay at the end of an anthology of Peirce's essays (including "Evolutionary Love") in 1923. In this article Dewey carefully selects those portions of Peirce's pragmaticism which seem to reinforce Dewey's experimental empiricism—and he ignores the rest. At the end of his essay Dewey says that "recourse to Peirce would . . . have a most beneficial influence in contemporary discussion," for "our epistemological difficulties arise from an attempt to define the 'real' as something given prior to reflective inquiry instead of as that which reflective inquiry is forced to reach and to which when it is reached belief can stably cling."[29] Of course this is the way that Peirce's "Neglected Argument" works, with its "certain lines of reflection which will inevitably suggest the hypothesis of God's Reality"; but such an hypothesis is certainly not one which, in Dewey's opinion, "reflective inquiry is forced to reach and to which when it is reached belief can stably cling." Why, then, does Dewey advocate "recourse to Peirce" as "a most beneficial influence in contemporary discussion," or at least why does Dewey not say openly that he and Peirce come to quite different ultimate conclusions by following the path of scientific inquiry?[30]

Dewey's treatment of Peirce might be compared to the treatment of Kant by most modern neo-Kantians, or to the treatment of Kierkegaard by modern atheistic existentialists; but the neo-Kantians, while concentrating on *The Critique of Pure Reason*, deplore what they consider to be the aberration of the Kant who wrote *The Critique of Practical Reason*, while the atheistic existentialists dismiss as a "failure of nerve" Kierkegaard's "leap of faith" after his early period of despair. The difference is that Dewey writes almost as if the Peirce of the Neglected Argument and other aspects of the "physical metaphysics" simply did not exist. Dewey does quote one of Peirce's statements that synechism (the principle of continuity) "is first shown to be true with mathematical exactitude in the field of logic, and is thence inferred to hold good metaphysically,"[31] but he never indicates that "the metaphysics of synechism" and other aspects of Peirce's metaphysics are more than an (easily ignored) excrescence on the philosophy of naturalism. "Summing up," says Dewey, "we may say that Peirce's pragmaticism is a doctrine concerning the meaning, conception, or rational purpose of objects, namely, that these consist in the 'effects, which might conceivably have practical bearings, we conceive the object of our conception to have. Then, our conception of these effects is the whole of our conception of the object.' "[32]

Dewey's summation would have been correct if he had implied that the most important effects are those deriving from the meta-physical portions of Peirce's pragmaticism.[33] But Dewey would have agreed completely with Sidney Hook that "it is demonstrable that no set of metaphysical or theological statements by themselves entail any specific empirical consequences about the life of man or the structure of human society."[34] Therefore, to repeat, Dewey is dis-torting Pierce's pragmaticism, as does Hook again and again—as, for example, in the following statement: "There is something ironical in the plea made by the professional misunderstanders of pragmaticism (a philosophy which in Peirce and Dewey is an explication of the logic and ethics of scientific method), for a revival of religion as a bulwark against totalitarianism."[35] Of course, Peirce was unorthodox with his combination of realism and "Schelling-fashioned idealism"; but he believed in a transcendent God, "a personal creator," as he frequently says. For example, we have the following statement: "a genuine evolutionary philosophy, that is, one that makes the principle of growth a primordial element of the universe, is so far from being antagonistic to the idea of a personal creator that it is really inseparable from that idea. . . ."[36]

It might be said that Dewey's article entitled "Peirce's Theory of Quality" is an exception to our statement about his attitude to Peirce, since, in challenging Professor Thomas A. Goudge's criticism of Peirce on the nature of the "given," Dewey does qualify his admiration by saying: "While he [Peirce] introduces at times (and rather unfortunately in my opinion) his pre-dilection for pan-psychic metaphysics, he is not writing on a metaphysical or cosmological basis, but is giving a logical analysis of experience. . . ." By this reference to Peirce's "pan-psychic predilections," Dewey means that Pierce "makes the immediate quality of *things* to be of the nature of feelings" and believes that, "*apart* from experience and phenomenology, the universe is constituted out of relations between something very like feelings and acts of effort-resistance, while natural continuity is inherently assimilable to what presents itself in experience as reflective thought." Even here Dewey says that Peirce's panpsychism is not "essential to his theory" and is not implied in his logical analysis and that this analysis has "opened the road which permits a truly experimental philosophy to be developed which does not, like traditional empirical philosophies, cut experience off from nature. . . . "[37] Dewey is, then, very carefully selecting the parts which "open the road" to his own type of "experimental philosophy"; and, if one depended on Dewey's interpretation alone (even including this article of qualified praise), he would still not learn that Peirce considered the merits of his theory of logical analysis to be "greatest in its application to the highest metaphysical principles,"[38] which include far more than what Dewey briefly refers to (as if they were an incidental excrescence) as Peirce's "pan-psychic predilections."

There is additional evidence that Dewey distorted Peirce when he failed to note that Peirce really intended his whole scheme of pragmaticism as a reinforcement of the "Neglected Argument" for a transcendent God. Besides Peirce's argument in *Collected Papers* (VI, 326-33), and elsewhere, the following from Volume I seems especially significant:

> The starting point of the Universe, God the Creator, is the Absolute First; the terminus of the Universe, God completely revealed, is the Absolute Second; every state of the Universe at a measurable point of time is the Third. If you think the measurable is all there is, and deny it any definite tendency whence or whither, then you are considering the pair of points that makes the absolute to be imaginary and are an Epicurean. If you hold that there is a definite drift to the course of of nature as a whole, but yet believe its absolute end is nothing but the Nirvana from which it set out, you make the two points of the absolute to be coincident, and are a pessimist. But if your creed is that the whole universe is approaching in the infinitely distant future a state having a general character different from that toward which we look back in the infinitely distant past, you make the absolute to consist in two distinct real points and are an evolutionist.[39]

This general character will be "an absolutely perfect, rational, and symmetrical system, in which mind is at last crystallized in the infinitely distant future."[40] The similarity of this cosmic interpretation of evolution to that of Chardin is obvious. Why Dewey failed to blast this part of Peirce's argument, which no naturalist could consider valid, is hard to understand, especially in view of his sharp attacks on any form of the transcendent appearing in the works of other philosophers.

Almost all the naturalistic philosophers besides Dewey who have noted Peirce's cosmic interpretation of evolution have found his logic to be in conflict with his metaphysics. Typical of such attacks on Peirce's metaphysics is the following by Professor Philip Wiener. After quoting Peirce's idea that "Metaphysics ought to be founded on logic. To found logic on metaphysics is a crazy scheme," Wiener says that "some such 'crazy scheme' has to be imputed to Peirce himself when in his speculative moods he attempted to explain the history of scientific thought and of logic by means of a cosmic evolutionism in which the laws of nature themselves evolve continuously in a world whose laws can only enjoy a contingent status."[41] This statement is certainly an oversimplification of Peirce's ideas both on "synechism" (continuity) and "tychism" (contingency or chance). Wiener does quote the following statement in which Peirce qualifies his definition of synechism: "Synechism is not an ultimate and metaphysical doctrine; it is a regulative principle of logic, prescribing what sort of hypothesis is fit to be entertained and examined."[42] Wiener says, however, that this qualification is inconsistent with "the second (metaphysical) use Peirce made of the idea of continuity," which includes 'objective idealism'. . . .[43]

In other words, according to Wiener, Peirce is attempting to say that continuity both is and is not an ultimate and metaphysical doctrine. But Wiener does not notice that Peirce has protected himself on this point in the following way: on the page preceding the statement that continuity is not an ultimate and metaphysical doctrine, he has said that, although synechism can be explained, still "the synechist cannot deny that there is an element of the inexplicable and ultimate, because it is directly forced upon him; nor does he abstain from generalizing from this experience. True generality is, in fact, nothing but a rudimentary form of true continuity."[44] Thus certainly Peirce is approaching the metaphysical doctrine from the standpoint of a preceding logic (based on experience) instead of making the "crazy" reversal (with logic based on metaphysics) attributed to him by Wiener. "The very reality [of the metaphysical doctrine], is his [the synechist's] way of looking at the matter," Peirce adds, "is nothing else than the way in which facts must ultimately come to be understood." "There would be a contradiction here," Peirce admits, "if this ultimacy were looked upon as something to be absolutely realized. . . ."[45] Thus when

Peirce says in the next sentence that "Synechism is not an ultimate and absolute metaphysical doctrine; it is a regulative principle of logic. . . ," he means simply that, although he believes in it as a metaphysical doctrine, since he has "generalized from an experience . . . directly forced upon him," still "the very reality" has not been "absolutely realized." This approach is similar to that of Kant to the "regulative" ideas of God, freedom, and immortality, in which Kant believed though he could not claim them as (presently) verifiable knowledge.

Wiener likewise failed to note the way in which Peirce explains how chance may be compatible with continuity: "I make use of chance [says Peirce] chiefly to make room for a principle of generalization, or tendency to form habits, which I hold has produced all regularities. The mechanical philosopher leaves the whole specification of the world utterly unaccounted for, which is pretty nearly as bad as to baldly attribute it to chance. I attribute it altogether to chance, it is true, but to chance in the form of a spontaneity which is to some degree regular."[46]

The "chance in the form of a spontaneity which is to some degree regular" is explained further in his essay on "Evolutionary Love" as a spontaneity which "is conferred upon the forms preserved" in evolution so that they are "drawn into harmony with their original [God], quite after the Christian scheme." Thus "just as love cannot have a contrary, but must embrace what is opposed to it, so tychasm [fortuitous variation] is a kind of agapasm [creative love]":[47] "The agapastic development of thought [he adds] is the adoption of certain mental tendencies, not altogether heedlessly, as in tychasm [non-agapastic tychasm he means], nor quite blindly by the mere force of circumstances or of logic, as in anancasm [mechanical necessity], but by an immediate attraction for the idea itself, whose nature is divined before the mind possesses it by the power of sympathy, that is, by virtue of the continuity of mind. . . ."[48]

Even if Wiener would admit that he had oversimplified Peirce's explanation of the relation between continuity and contingency, he would no doubt still reject the full development of the argument in the manner briefly indicated by the above quotations, and so, one would suppose, would Dewey (in spite of his not refuting Peirce). The naturalist thinks he is perfectly justified in accepting, for example, both the contradictory theories of light since strong evidence seems to prove that light is composed of waves and equally strong evidence seems to prove that it is composed of particles, but he condemns as illogical the philosopher who argues for both fortuitous variation and divine creative love in evolution.

Peirce saw no contradiction (and there really is none) between his theism and his emphasis on the scientific method for solving all problems that could be solved by this method. As he said, "Pragmaticism . . . implies faith in common sense and instinct, though only as they issue from the cupel-furnace of measured criticism. In short, . . . the N.A. [Neglected Argument] is the First Stage of a scientific inquiry, resulting in a hypothesis of the very highest Plausibility, whose ultimate test must lie in its value in the self-controlled growth of man's conduct of life."[49] As part of this scientific inquiry he developed his theory of tychasm (or chance) which, he said, "must give birth to an evolutionary cosmology, in which all the regularities of nature and of mind are regarded as products of growth, and to a Schelling-fashioned idealism which holds matter to be mere specialized and partially deadened mind."[50] Before this theory of objective idealism can be accepted, however, he says, "it must show itself capable of explaining the tri-dimensionality of space, the laws of motion, and the general characteristics of the universe, with mathematical precision; for no less should be demanded of every philosophy."[51]

We shall not attempt to show how Peirce attempted to accomplish all of his tremendous task (for a detailed explanation of his whole system would take another book); it is sufficient here to consider one of his main essays (from which we have already quoted briefly), "Evolutionary Love," which appeared in *The Monist* in 1893 and was reprinted in the anthology entitled *Chance, Love, and Logic* (1949) as well as in the *Collected Papers*. This essay is selected because its evolutionary cosmology is in most respects very similar to that of Teilhard de Chardin in *The Phenomenon of Man*, and because these works of Peirce and Chardin indicate that the theory of evolution, contrary to the argument of Dewey, can be convincingly interpreted as reinforcing belief in a trancendent God.[52] Both Peirce and Chardin knew considerably more about science than did Dewey; in fact, they were both distinguished scientists as well as philosophers.

Peirce distinguishes three types of evolution for which claims have been made: evolution by fortuitous variation (or tychasm), evolution by mechanical necessity (anancasm), and evolution by creative love (agapasm). He maintains that

> . . . tychasm and anancasm are degenerate forms of agapasm.
>
> Men who seek to reconcile the Darwinian idea with Christianity will remark that tychastic evolution, like the agapastic, depends upon a reproductive creation, the forms preserved being those that use the spontaneity conferred upon them in such wise as to be drawn into harmony with their original, quite after the Christian scheme. Very good! This only shows that just as love cannot have a contrary, but must embrace what is opposed to it, so tychasm is a kind of agapasm. . . . The agapastic development of thought is the adoption of certain mental tendencies, not altogether heedlessly, as in tychasm, not quite blindly by the mere force of circumstances or of logic, as in anancasm, but by an immediate attraction for the idea itself, whose nature is divined before the mind possesses it by the power of sympathy, that is, by virtue of the continuity of mind. . . .[53]

This argument may be said, from one standpoint, to presuppose an "original," God, who "conferred spontaneity" upon the "forms," giving them, that is, freedom to use this gift "in such wise as to be drawn into harmony with their original"; but, from another standpoint, the reality of God was Peirce's conclusion drawn from the evidences of design in the universe. Even, however, if we consider Peirce's theism to be a presupposition, is not this argument quite as convincing as Dewey's "genetic" theory (with its opposite presupposition)—namely, that the whole process of evolution is sufficiently explained by the principle of inquiry (doubt, inquiry, resolution)—operating all the way from the groping adjustment to environment of the lowest forms up to the development of human thought? Dewey vacillates between the contention that this process generated itself and the "natural piety" of his giving most of the credit to Mother Nature. As an example of his argument that the process generated itself, consider this: "Organization is an empirical trait of some events, no matter how false are doctrines about it which have construed it as evidence of a special force or entity called life or soul."[54] As an example of his argument which gives Mother Nature most of the credit, consider this from the same book: "The striving of man for objects of imagination is a continuation of natural processes. . . . When he adds perception and ideas to these endeavors, it is not after all he who adds; the addition is again the doing of nature and a further complication of its own domain."[55]

IV *Chardin and Dewey: Superficial Similarity and Basic Contrast*

Chardin's theory of evolutionary continuity, although similar to Peirce's, is more fully developed and more specifically Christian, as will soon be apparent. Chardin first maintains that, even in the most rudimentary form of so-called inert matter, there is a primitive form of what later will become life or mind—a "Within" as well as a "Without".[56] "Looked at from *within*, as well as observed from *without*, the stuff of the universe thus tends . . . to be resolved backwardly into a dust of particles that are (i) perfectly alike among themselves (at least if they are observed from a great distance; (ii) each co-extensive with the whole of the cosmic realm; (iii) mysteriously connected among themselves, finally, by a comprehensive energy. In these depths the two aspects, external and internal, correspond point by point."[57]

This elementary stuff of the universe after a long span of time becomes the simplest form of protoplasm, which "is already a substance of unheard of complexity.[58] This complexity increases in geometrical progression as we pass from the protozoan higher and higher up the scale of the metazoa. And so it is for the whole of the remainder always and everywhere. . . . Spiritual perfection (or conscious 'centreity') and material synthesis (or complexity) are but the two aspects or connected parts of one and the same phenomenon."[59] So far, Chardin's speculations about evolution are not unlike those of Dewey, and Dewey would certainly have agreed with most of the following statement: "by the very fact of the individualisation of our planet, a certain mass of elementary consciousness was originally emprisoned in the matter of earth. . . . By its initial chemical composition, the early earth is itself, and in its totality, the incredibly complex germ we are seeking. Congenitally, if I may use the word, it already carried pre-life within it, and this moreover in *definite quantity*."[60]

Dewey might have objected to some of the wording here (especially "mass of elementary consciousness") as too suggestive of a kind of panpsychism, but otherwise he would have found this passage and most of the rest of *Phenomenon* to be a reinforcement of his naturalism. Even more specific (if Dewey were looking for such reinforcement) is the following passage: "The earth was probably born by accident; but, in accordance with one of the most general laws of evolution, scarcely had this accident happened than it was immediately made use of and recast into someting *naturally directed* [italics mine]."[61] Indeed, we can well imagine Dewey writing an essay on Chardin in which (as he did in his discussion of Peirce) he would concentrate upon passages like these that seem (out of context) to reinforce his own naturalism.

Chardin deliberately omitted references to the religious aspects of his evolutionary philosophy until toward the end of his book because, as he said, he wanted his book read "purely and simply as a scientific treatise."[62] This would be in the spirit of Peirce's idea that "metaphysics ought to be founded on logic."[63] After tracing the long ascent toward consciousness, however, Chardin says that evolution "should culminate forwards in some sort of supreme consciousness."[64] This further development which he prophesies, he calls a "noogenesis," in which

> . . . time and space become truly humanised—or rather superhumanised. Far from being mutually exclusive, the Universal and Personal (that is to say the "centred") grow in the same direction and culminate simultaneously in each other.
>
> It is therefore a mistake to look for the extension of our being or of the noosphere in the Impersonal. The Future-Universal could not be anything else but the Hyper-Personal—at the Omega Point.[65]

The "Hyper-Personal" here is no Nietzschean Superman but the God of Christianity, Who is not only the "Omega Point" of the ascent, but Who also (through the Incarnation) as "Christ, principle of universal vitality because sprung up as man among men, put himself in the position(maintained ever since) to subdue under himself, to purify, to direct and superanimate the general ascent of consciousness into which he inserted himself."[66]

It seems clear, then, that two of the greatest thinkers in modern times, both of them very learned in science(one a very distinguished paleontologist), have used the scientific method with all the thoroughness which Dewey could desire and have drawn from it ultimate conclusions about cosmology and metaphysics quite different from those of Dewey and his followers. One of the followers, Sidney Hook, for example, has said without qualification that "The religious renaissance of our time is really part of the more inclusive movement of irrationalism in modern thought."[67] Of course, Hook is a zealous follower who really outdoes the master in condemning religion; Hook is so suspicious of the word *God*, for example, that he disagrees with Dewey's use of it even to refer to a subjective projection of man's own ideas. Dewey himself, as we have seen, wants a religious renaissance but a strictly secularized religion which would evoke as much emotional fervor over the use of the scientific method (in his, not Peirce's and Chardin's interpretation of this phrase) as has been, and is being, generated by belief in a transcendent God.

V Trend in Modern Science Toward Belief in Transcendent God

There have been many distinguished modern scientists who have interpreted science not only as not in conflict with belief in a transcendent God but as really logically supporting such a belief. In fact, if we may trust the statements of a considerable number of them, the trend in recent years has been toward, rather than away from, this belief in God. Consider for example, Dr. Henry Margenau, professor of physics and natural philosophy at Yale, who said in 1958:

> It is clear that a rigid and final fixation of the metaphysical principles underlying science is neither necessary for the possibility nor exhibited in the course of science. . . .
>
> Constructs satisfying the principles of reason and also confirmed by empirical tests may be called verifacts. And the verifacts, or at least a certain definable class of them, compose within our experience the domain of physical reality.
>
> This is the end of the *epistemological* story, in which science is the primary actor. It leaves reality within experience and therefore stops short of Thomas's [St. Thomas Aquinas'] ontological position. I note this with emphasis, for it seems to me that beyond this point science is no longer a reliable guide . . . most scientists do believe that experience points to an ontological reality beyond the physical which consists only of verifacts. To reach ontological reality he [the scientist] must make a leap, a commitment of a kind transcending, I believe, those which enable him to be a scientist. He must indeed entrust himself to other hands. And here, it seems to me, Aquinas' doctrine of essences, his theory of the scale of being of substances serves useful purposes.[68]

Another prominent physicist, Professor Harold K. Schilling, confirms this view of the metaphysical implications of science in the following statement: "The conception being espoused by scientists today . . . views nature as a *world of depth*, not as a shallow one . . . as a *world of mystery* that is in the end not fathomable . . . science points beyond its own definitive findings toward the reality of ultimate mystery. . . ."[69]

The trend among scientists to which Professors Margenau and Schilling refer has of course grown much more since than before Dewey's death in 1952, but he could have observed it as far back as the 1920's in the work of prominent physicists like Arthur Eddington and James Jeans, and (still more notably) in the philosophical essays of one of the very greatest modern physicists, Werner Heisenberg. These essays (collected into a book entitled *Philosophic Problems of Nuclear Science* and published in 1952, the year of Dewey's death) began to appear as early as 1934. In 1949 Heisenberg said in a lecture at the University of Leipzig:

> . . . we probably understand now, better than before, that there exist apart from the phenomena of life, still other aspects of reality, i.e. consciousness and, finally, mental processes. We cannot expect that there should be a direct link between our understanding of the movement of bodies in space, and of the processes of the mind, since we have learnt from science that our mental approach to reality takes place, at first, on separate levels which link up, so to speak, only behind the phenomena in an abstract space. We are now more conscious that there is no definite initial point of view from which radiate routes into all fields of the perceptible, but that all perception must, so to speak, be suspended over an unfathomable depth.[70]

In a lecture at Göttingen University in 1946, Heisenberg departed still further from a position of which Dewey and his followers would have approved:

> The core of science is formed, to my mind, by the pure sciences, which are not concerned with practical applications. They are the branches in which pure thought attempts to discover the hidden harmonies of nature . . . it may be that people today will be satisfied to know that though the gate [to understanding the full implications of science] is not open to everyone there can be no deceit beyond the gate. We have no power there—the decisions are taken by a higher power." People have used different words at different times for this "centre." They called it "spirit" or "God," . . . There are many ways to this centre, even today, and science is only one of them.[71]

Sidney Hook, one of Dewey's most loyal followers, apparently had not read the above passages from Heisenberg; for he uses Heisenberg to bolster his attack on those scientists for whom the existence of God is indicated by the "harmony of natural law." Heisenberg and Neils Bohr, says Hook, "are not prepared to give the universe high marks for the order of rationality found in nuclear behavior."[72] Heisenberg's theory of indeterminacy certainly put an end to the deterministic physics that preceded him, but just as Peirce (also misinterpreted by Hook) found that tychasm and agapasm work together, so Heisenberg believes in "hidden harmonies of nature" which the pure sciences are "attempting to discover," and in this quest "there will be a final decision as to what is right and what is wrong. . . . There is a higher power, not influenced by our wishes, which finally decides and judges."[73] If Hook had read the essays of Heisenberg, he would have added him to the large list of those whom he finds guilty in this century of "The New Failure of Nerve." From Hook's point of view, he really should also have added Peirce; but, instead, in several places—just as Dewey ignored Peirce's metaphysics—he quotes from Peirce to bolster up his laborious argument for naturalism.

It is the acknowledgment of the "unfathomable depth," referred to by Heisenberg and the "mystery not in the end fathomable" referred to by Schilling, that distinguishes the religious attitude of a growing number of physicists in the twentieth century from the attitude of Dewey and other naturalists. As Professor Paul Roubiczek has said, "Physics has probably advanced farthest of all natural sciences. Modern physicists have discovered some kind of reality behind or beyond the reality with which we are confronted, a reality of a different kind which some of them call absolute."[74] It is almost certain that Dewey would not have been, and that his followers still living are not, impressed by the growing trend among scientists here reported. He would have dismissed it, as does Sidney Hook, as part of "The New Failure of Nerve", and he would have insisted, as does Hook, that naturalism "proposes to treat assertions about God's existence in the same generic way that it treats assertions about the existence of invisible stars or hidden motives or afterimages or extrasensory perception."[75]

Yet many persons who are neither confirmed naturalists nor confirmed believers in a transcendent God may be led to decide that, since (on such tremendous issues) no one can remain uncommitted to one side or the other, there is intellectual cogency as well as spiritual comfort in the "discovery" of modern physicists that there is "some kind of reality behind or beyond the reality with which we are confronted" and in the clear implication that this reality may well indicate a transcendent God. The naturalists do not believe in

130

Dewey and His Contemporaries

such a God because there is no experiment which can give us a description beyond one which is said to be "analogical" (and therefore not precise and scientifically verifiable). However, although it is likewise not precise and verifiable, they accept as true Ludwig Feuerbach's interpretation of God as the subjective projection of man's needs and care, since to them it seems more plausible. They are, then, illustrating the truth of the following statement of Professor Edwyn Bevan:

> You cannot, as some agnostics have supposed you can, keep simply to the ground of ascertained facts and make no leap off it into unprovable hypothesis. . . . Any hypothesis you adopt about the Ground of the world is a venture beyond experience, and yet the unarrestable advance of time pushes you, every moment of your conscious life, willy-nilly into action of some kind, and action necessarily presupposes some hypothesis regarding the Ground of the Universe. You are not securing yourself against the possibility of mistake if you decide to act on the hypothesis that there is no God, that the Ground of the Universe is wholly indifferent to the values which the spirit of man recognizes. You are acting just as much on an unproved hypothesis as the man who adjusts his action to belief that God is. And your action may turn out to have been defective because your hypothesis was wrong. . . . If you determine to live by the faith that the Ground of the universe is Spirit, and that the values which man recognizes are the revelation of that Spirit's character, there is likely to be more buoyancy and drive in your fight for goodness and truth and beauty, in the world around you and in yourself, against all the things which militate for wrong and falsehood and ugliness.[76]

If this argument of Bevan seems to mix too much of the prudential with the spiritual (somewhat after the manner of Pascal's famous "wager"), it may at least make a good beginning toward breaking out of the very constricted boundaries of naturalism and humanism, which Richard Niebuhr has called "exclusive systems of closed societies"—their narrowness the very evil against which they are supposed to protest. "Genuinely radical monotheism," says Niebuhr,

> . . . has included all that humanism includes and something more. It has affirmed not only all mankind but all being. It has involved men not only in battle against the wrongs that afflict men but set them into

131

conflict with what is destructive and anarchic in all accessible realms of being. Its religion has found holiness in man, but also in all nature and in what is beyond nature. It has believed in the salvation of men from evil, but also in the liberation of the whole groaning and travailing creation. Its science has sought to understand men, yet for it the proper study of mankind has been not only man but the infinitely great and the infinitely small in the whole realm of being. . . .

Radical monotheism as the gift of confidence in the principle of being itself, as the affirmation of the real, as loyalty—betrayed and reconstructed many times—to the universe of being, can have no quarrel with humanism and naturalism insofar as these are protests against the religions and ethics of closed societies, centering in little gods— or in little ideas of God. But insofar as faith is given to men in the principle of being itself, or insofar as they are reconciled to the Determiner of Destiny as the fountain of good and only of good, naturalism and humanism assume the form of exclusive systems of closed societies.[77]

To those who, like Dewey in his self-reliant moods, think that "Man is capable, if he will but exercise the required courage, intelligence, and effort, of shaping his own fate"[78]—this reference to a transcendent Determiner of Destiny will appear to be pure verbiage. Such Deweyites include those who, like Hook, stake almost all on the intellect, and those who, like Geiger (following the master more closely), add a secular religion promising the "emotional fire and revolutionary power of man's faith in man."[79] In his cosmic drama moods (as we have seen) Dewey's religion, though still scornful of the Transcendent in any form, went beyond that of most of his followers to include a reliance on Nature as the "infinite" which is "behind us" and which has formed us from our humblest beginnings to the addition of consciousness and intellect.

In *Experience and Nature*, Dewey wrote that "The striving of man for objects of imagination is a continuation of natural processes. . . . When he adds perception and ideas to these endeavors, it is not after all he who adds; the addition is again the doing of nature and a further complication of its own domain."[80] But this attitude toward nature is still naturalism; and, as we have shown, an increasing number of the greatest modern scientists and philosophers (all of whom knew or know more about science than Dewey knew) have found naturalism, even with Dewey's semi-pantheistic "natural piety," insufficient to explain the mystery which deepens as scientific knowledge advances. Most scientists are now willing to grant what Gabriel Marcel has maintained[81]—that there are mysteries which science can never penetrate as well as problems which will be solved with future scientific research.

In this respect, Roubiczek's statement (verified by most prominent scientists) is worth repeating: "Modern physics has probably advanced farthest of all natural sciences. Modern physicists have discovered some kind of reality behind or beyond the reality with which we are confronted, a reality of a different kind. . . . The physicist must admit that there is a reality which, though it can be ascertained, can no longer be understood, or as Heisenberg has put it, that all such knowledge is 'suspended over an unfathomable depth.'"[82] And, concerning this transcendent realm, Heisenberg, reflecting on the implications of his studies in physics, has said: "We have no power there—the decisions are taken by a higher power."[83]

It would seem highly significant that science has at last recognized the truth of what Pascal said at a time when human reason was thought to be supreme: "The last proceeding of reason is to recognize that there is an infinity of things which are beyond it. It is but feeble if it does not see so far as to know this."[84] Pascal is not saying that we should "offend the principle of reason," because if we do so, "our religion will be absurd and ridiculous."[85] But he does say (and this concept would follow from his statement about "the last proceeding of reason"): "We know truth, not only by the reason, but also by the heart, and it is in this last way that we know first principles."[86]

CHAPTER 9

Dewey in the History
of American Thought

E VEN those most opposed to naturalistic monism as a philosophy cannot deny that Dewey has been one of the most influential thinkers of this century. None but the blindest of his followers can deny that his influence has declined considerably in the seventeen years since his death in 1952. Our conclusion must be an effort, therefore, to account for both these facts.

In the first place, his contribution to educational theory was sufficient to make him famous. Although indebted to great predecessors such as Rousseau and Pestalozzi, Dewey was in an important sense the founder and continued to be the leader of the most important change in secondary education in this century, "progressive education." He was also among those who condemned its eventual excesses and helped to perpetuate the sound aspects of this movement. To be sure, his own educational theory was excessively dependent on the scientific method, which became to him a panacea for all ills. That such a bias in Dewey was in part responsible for the excesses that developed in progressive education should not, however, diminish the credit due him for his common-sense detection of such failures as lack of organization and discipline in many of the progressive schools.

Inseparable from his contribution to American educational theory is his important contribution, both in his writings and in his active leadership of reform movements, to the progress of democracy in this country. In organizations whose aim was to remove injustices suffered by teachers both at the secondary and university levels, Dewey was a leader both nationally and internationally. He lectured at universities in various foreign countries—including Japan, China, and Russia—in a well-received effort to improve educational procedures and promote international good will. That he misunderstood some of the rapidly changing conditions in some of these countries and that his work, especially in China and Russia, did not eventually seem to succeed very well should not detract from the sincerity of his efforts or from the considerable value of the books and articles that he published about conditions in these countries when he visited them.

In spite of some disagreement on details about his contribution to education and democracy, Dewey's position as a leader in these two closely connected fields, then, has not been seriously challenged. But in the more speculative realms of philosophy, especially the cosmic implications of his experimental naturalism, where Dewey hoped to make his major contribution, he met much opposition (although he gained much loyal support) both in the details and in the major premises of his attempt to reconstruct metaphysics and to reduce it to a new combination of experience and nature. In fact, as one of his most ardent supporters, Richard J. Bernstein, admits, serious and widespread disagreement with various aspects of Dewey's position began with the criticisms of his early *Studies in Logical Theory* (1903). Bernstein then adds significantly: "Dewey was forced to clarify, explicate, and defend his position, a task which occupied him for the rest of his life."[1]

The liveliness of the controversy is perhaps best illustrated in the Schilpp volume, which appeared in two editions. The opposition of even some of Dewey's fellow naturalists, most notably Santayana and Russell (both of whom wrote rather superficial essays in this volume), is perhaps due to their not taking the trouble to penetrate the ragged obscurity of his prose style. Dewey, a skillful controversialist, disposed of their objections rather easily; but other naturalists, most notably Reichenbach, found flaws which gave Dewey more trouble. Such, as we have noted earlier, is Reichenbach's objection to Dewey's attempt to make emotions qualities of things. Reichenbach maintains that affective (emotional) qualities are not "*qualities* of things, but *relations* between thing and observer, varying therefore with the nature of observer." Dewey's rather unsatisfactory answer to Reichenbach is that "as distinct from the position taken by Mr. Reichenbach there is no inherent theoretical bar on my view to some day succeeding."[2]

Such an answer indicates one important flaw in Dewey's tactics as a powerful polemicist—a tendency, when hard pressed on his own terms, to retreat into vague prophecies concerning a time when his views will be vindicated. This sentence answering Reichenbach is typical also of a kind of knotty syntax noticeable in too many of Dewey's sentences. As Professor Warner Berthoff has well said,

> An inspiring teacher, he [Dewey] was also a remarkably careless writer; one whose instinct for right-minded catch phrases was stronger than his feelings for precise usage; a critic and publicist who too often carried out his attack on unexamined assumptions with unexamined verbal equipment. . . . Edmund Wilson has recalled, from his work as literary editor of *The New Republic*, the "peculiarly exasperating way" in which Dewey's contributions "both called for and resisted revision": "It was not only a question of clarifying the author's statements but of finding out what he meant, and when you did get the sense of this meaning, there was no way of straightening out the language: you would have had to try to give his meaning in a language of a different kind."[3]

But Dewey's verbal obscurity is not in itself enough to account for the decline in his reputation since his death in 1952. A more important reason, as I have tried to demonstrate in the preceding chapter, has been the increasing realization of a number of the most eminent scientists that, to quote Heisenberg, "there is no definite initial point of view from which radiate routes into all fields of the perceptible, but that all perception must, so to speak, be suspended over an unfathomable depth"[4] beyond the reach of either science or nature—a mystery which is not in the end fathomable and which therefore may well lead to religious faith.

There are, of course, many who still agree with and follow Dewey rather than Heisenberg on the above point, and who do not feel that Dewey's reputation has declined in any way. Much special interest and publicity, including numerous articles, marked the celebration in 1959 of the centennial of his birth. The Dewey Center at Southern Illinois University, where several distinguished Dewey scholars are located, is now well on its way to publishing a definitive edition of all his voluminous writings, part of which will no doubt be studied for many years to come.

Another important aspect of Dewey's appeal to many in this century has been his promise of solutions to spiritual problems that have troubled them. Dewey assures those who have lost religious faith that they can be religious without having a religion, that they can even have a God whom they can conveniently interpret as no more than the projection of their own wonderful minds. In Dewey's opinion, mind, though wonderful, is a function of matter; and knowing is a purely natural event no more mysterious than any other operation of nature. His account of knowledge is usually limited to the description of a pattern of inquiry, which is itself loosely patterned upon procedures in the composition of a work of art. One's moral problems, according to Dewey, can be solved by a process exactly parellel to, and quite as successful as, the scientific method in our awe-inspiring technology, a method involving experimentation and an assessment of consequences with a "continuum of inquiry." This kind of approach to moral and spiritual problems Dewey calls the true, as contrasted with Kant's mistaken, "Copernican revolution" in philosophy. It is no wonder that many who considered themselves to be the intellectual elite of the modern world flocked to the banner thus appealingly hoisted.

I have tried in this book to give the general reader a reasonable and fair introduction to Dewey's philosophy, but I have felt at the same time obliged to call attention to its serious limitations, which have become more and more apparent in the years since his voluminous writings had the support of his powerful personality in inspiring his disciples to spread his gospel abroad. Hero worship for some of these has been replaced by discriminating reappraisal; and, since his death, not many converts have been added.

Notes and References

Chapter One

1. Dewey, "From Absolutism to Experimentalism" in Richard J. Bernstein (ed.) *John Dewey: On Experience, Nature, and Freedom* (New York, 1960), p. 5.
2. Max Eastman, "John Dewey," *The Atlantic Monthly*, CLXVIII (December, 1941), 673.
3. "From Absolutism to Experimentalism," pp. 10-11.
4. Quoted in Morton White, *The Origin of Dewey's Instrumentalism* (New York, 1943), p. 93.
5. John Blewett, "Democracy in Religion: Unity in Human Relations," in John Blewett (ed.), *John Dewey: His Thoughts and Influence* (New York, 1960), p. 41.
6. Jane Dewey, "Biography of John Dewey," P. A. Schilpp (ed.), *The Philosophy of John Dewey* (New York, 1951), p. 21.
7. White, p. 151.
8. *Logic: The Theory of Inquiry* (New York, 1938), p. iii.
9. Richard J. Bernstein, Introduction in Bernstein (ed.), *John Dewey: On Experience, Nature, and Freedom*, p. xix.
10. Cf. Blewett's essay referred to in Note 5.
11. Jane Dewey, "Biography of John Dewey," p. 39.
12. *Ibid.*, p. 42.
13. *Ibid.*, p. 43.
14. *Ibid.*, p. 44.
15. For most of the information about Dewey's family I am indebted to Mrs. Joanna Boydston, editor of the projected complete edition of Dewey's works now being published at the Dewey Center at Southern Illinois University.

Chapter Two

1. John Blewett, "Democracy as Religion: Unity in Human Relations," in John Blewett (ed.), *John Dewey: His Thought and Influence*, p. 37.
2. "The Significance of the Problem of Knowledge," in John Dewey, *The Influence of Darwin on Philosophy and Other Essays in Contemporary Thought* (New York, 1910), pp. 271-304.
3. *Ibid.*, pp. 285-86.
4. *Ibid.*, p. 287. If this passage reminds us of Emerson's "Self-Reliance," it is not surprising when we recall the often quoted passage in one of

Dewey's other early essays in which he calls Emerson "the one citizen of the New World fit to have his name uttered in the same breath with that of Plato."—"Ralph Waldo Emerson," John Dewey, *Characters and Events,* ed. Joseph Ratner (New York, 1929), I, 76.

5. "The Significance of the Problem of Knowledge," p. 299.

6. *Ibid.,* p. 301.

7. *Experience and Nature* (New York, 1929), pp. 258, 261.

8. " 'Consciousness' and Experience," *The Influence of Darwin on Philosophy,* pp. 242-270.

9. *Ibid.,* p. 255.

10. *Ibid.,* p. 263.

11. "Beliefs and Existences," *The Influence of Darwin on Philosophy,* pp. 169-97.

12. *Ibid.,* pp. 188-89.

13. p. 189.

14. "The Influence of Darwinism on Philosophy," *The Influence of Darwin on Philosophy,* pp. 1-19.

15. *Ibid.,* p. 14.

16. *Ibid.,* p. 13.

17. Charles Darwin, *The Origin of Species and The Descent of Man* New York, n.d.), p. 374.

18. *Ibid.,* p. 468.

19. Quoted in Francis Darwin (ed.), *The Life and Letters of Charles Darwin* (New York, 1959), I, 282.

20. *Experience and Nature,* pp. 419, 420.

21. "The Subject Matter of Metaphysical Inquiry," in Richard J. Bernstein (ed.), *John Dewey, On Experience, Nature, and Freedom,* pp. 211-23.

22. "The Influence of Darwinism on Philosophy," p. 14.

23. "The Subject Matter of Metaphysical Inquiry," pp. 222-23.

24. *Ibid.,* p. 222.

25. *Ibid.,* p. 216.

26. *Experience and Nature.* pp. 421-22.

27. John Dewey and Others, *Studies in Logical Theory* (Chicago, 1903).

28. Morton White, *The Origin of Dewey's Instrumentalism, passim.*

29. *Studies in Logical Theory,* pp. 43-44.

30. White, p. 137.

31. "The Reflex Arc Concept in Psychology," *Psychological Review,* III (1896), 357-70.

32. *Studies in Logical Theory,* p. 24.

33. *Ibid.,* p. 25.

34. "From Absolutism to Experimentalism," p. 12.

35. *Ibid.,* p. 13.

36. *Moral Philosophy* (New York, 1964), p. 401.

37. *How We Think* (Boston, 1909).

38. *Logic: The Theory of Inquiry* (New York, 1938).
39. *The Influence of Darwin on Philosophy*, pp. 267-68.
40. *Democracy and Education* (New York, 1929), p. 101.
41. *Ibid.*, p. 80.
42. *Ibid.*, p. 394.
43. *Ibid.*, pp. 160, 161.
44. Sister Joseph Mary Raby, "John Dewey and Progressive Education," in John Blewett (ed.), *John Dewey: His Thought and Influence*, p. 111
45. *Democracy and Education*, p. 418.
46. "John Dewey and Progressive Education," p. 109.
47. *Experience and Education* (New York, 1938), p. 22.
48. *Ibid.*, p. 93.
49. *Democracy and Education*, pp. 160, 161.
50. John Blewett, "Democracy as Religion: Unity in Human Relations," p. 52.
51. "From Absolutism to Experimentalism," p. 18.

Chapter Three

1. *Experience and Nature*, p. 8.
2. *Ibid.*, p. 4a.
3. *Ibid.*, p. 25.
4. *Ibid.*, p. 28.
5. *Ibid.*, p. 422.
6. *Ibid.*, p. 28.
7. *Ibid.*, p. 39.
8. John Herman Randall, Jr., "Dewey's Interpretation of the History of Philosophy," P. A. Schilpp (ed.) *The Philosophy of John Dewey*, p. 102.
9. *Experience and Nature*, p. 48.
10. *Ibid.*, p. 50.
11. *Ibid.*
12. J. H. Bernard (ed.) *Kant's Critique of Judgment (London, 1931)*, p. 371.
13. *Experience and Nature*, p. 50.
14. "From Absolutism to Experimentalism," in Bernstein (ed.), John Dewey, *On Experience, Nature, and Freedom*, p. 13.
15. *Experience and Nature*, p. 54.
16. *Ibid.*, p. 56.
17. *Ibid.*, p. 59.
18. *Ibid.*
19. John Dewey and James H. Tufts, *Ethics* (New York, 1908), Chapter VI, especially p. 109: "The Hebrews presented the ideal of a moral order on earth, of a control of all life by right, of a realization of good, and of a completeness of life. It was an ideal not dreamed out in ecstatic visions of pure fancy, but worked out in struggle and suffering. . . . The ideal order is

to be made real. The divine kingdom is to come, the divine will be done 'on earth as it is in heaven.' "

20. *Experience and Nature*, p. 57, quoting Bertrand Russell.
21. *Ibid.*, p. 62.
22. In Bernstein (ed.), John Dewey, *On Experience, Nature and Freedom*, p. 12.
23. *Experience and Nature*, p. 116.
24. *Ibid.*, p. 118.
25. *Ibid.*, pp. 24-25.
26. Hans Reichenbach, "Dewey's Theory of Science," in Paul Arthur Schilpp (ed.), *The Philosophy of John Dewey*, pp. 179-80.
27. John Dewey, "Experience, Knowledge, and Value: A Rejoinder," in Paul Arthur Schilpp (ed.), *The Philosophy of John Dewey*, p. 543.
28. *Experience and Nature*, p. 422.
29. Reichenbach, "Dewey's Theory of Science," in Paul Arthur Schilpp (ed.), *The Philosophy of John Dewey*, p. 181.
30. *Experience and Nature*, p. 67.
31. *Ibid.*, p. 76.
32. *Ibid.*
33. *Ibid.*, p. 421.
34. *Ibid.*, p. 422.
35. *Ibid.*, p. 84.
36. *Ibid.*, p. 78.
37. *Ibid.*, p. 86.
38. *Ibid.*, p. 116.
39. *Ibid.*, p. 118.
40. In his autobiographical essay Dewey said of himself that, in his thinking after he abandoned his early adherence to a kind of Hegelianism, he "seemed to be unstable, chameleon-like, yielding one after another to many diverse and even incompatible influences." "From Absolutism to Experimentalism," in Richard J. Bernstein (ed.), John Dewey, *On Experience, Nature, and Freedom*, p. 13.
41. *Experience and Nature*, p. 119.
42. *Ibid.*, p. 127.
43. *Ibid.*
44. *Ibid.*, p. 92.
45. *Ibid.*, p. 94.
46. *Ibid.*, p. 92.
47. *Ibid.*, p. 95.
48. *Ibid.*, p. 98.
49. *Ibid.*, p. 100.
50. *Ibid.*, p. 133.
51. *Ibid.*, p. 135.
52. *Ibid.*, p. 137.

53. *Ibid.*, p. 154.
54. *Ibid.*, pp. 184-85.
55. *Ibid.*, pp. 170-71.
56. *Ibid.*, p. 183.
57. *Ibid.*, p. 186.
58. *Ibid.*, p. 172.
59. *Ibid.*, p. 222.
60. *Ibid.*, p. 230.
61. *Ibid.*, p. 225.
62. *Ibid.*, p. 242.
63. *Ibid.*
64. *Ibid.*
65. *Ibid.*, p. 245.
66. *Ibid.*, pp. 245-46.
67. *Ibid.*, p. 247.
68. *Ibid.*, p. 255.
69. *Ibid.*
70. *Ibid.*
71. *Ibid.*, pp. 258, 261.
72. *Ibid.*, pp. 265-66.
73. Lester E. Dennon (ed.), *Bertrand Russell's Dictionary of Mind, Matter and Morals* (New York, 1952), p. 160.
74. *Experience and Nature*, pp. 276, 279.
75. *Ibid.*, p. 285.
76. *Ibid.*
77. Ibid., p. 295.
78. *Ibid.*, pp. 295, 297.
79. *Ibid.*, p. 301.
80. *Ibid.*, p. 306.
81. Alfred North Whitehead, *Adventures of Ideas* (New York, 1935), p. 305.
82. *Experience and Nature*, p. 331.
83. *Ibid.*
84. *Ibid.*, p. 247.
85. *Ibid.*, p. 343.
86. *Ibid.*, p. 350.
87. *Ibid.*, p. 353.
88. *Ibid.*, p. 358. Dewey apparently here (where he makes art "the complete culmination of nature") would consider the "esthetic vision" as a subdivision of complete art, but this still will not resolve the contradiction, because in the earlier statement the advent of the "esthetic vision" meant quite simply that "knowing has stepped out of the picture," p. 331.
89. *Ibid.*, p. 358.
90. *Ibid.*, pp. 360, 361.

91. *Ibid.*, p. 378.
92. *Ibid.*, p. 379.
93. *Ibid.*, pp. 383-84.
94. *Ibid.*, pp. 376-77.
95. *Ibid.*, pp. 117-18.
96. *Ibid.*, p. 377.
97. Dewey never capitalizes *classicism*, and he is inconsistent in capitalizing *Romanticism* in referring to a type of art.
98. *Experience and Nature*, p. 118.
99. *Ibid.*, p. 391.
100. *Ibid.*, pp. 398-99.
101. *Ibid.*, p. 400.
102. *Ibid.*, p. 78.
103. *Ibid.*, p. 401.
104. *Ibid.*, p. 406.
105. *Ibid.*, p. 407.
106. *Ibid.*, p. 412.
107. *Ibid.*, p. 413.
108. *Ibid.*, p. 421.
109. *Ibid.*, p. 420.
110. *Ibid.*, p. 419.

Chapter Four

1. *Reconstruction in Philosophy* (New York, 1950), p. 8.
2. *Ibid.*, p. 10.
3. *Ibid.*, p. 27.
4. *Ibid.*
5. *Ibid.*
6. *Ibid.*, p. 28.
7. *The Quest for Certainty* (New York, 1929).
8. *Ibid.*, p. 84.
9. *Ibid.*, p. 87.
10. *Reconstruction in Philosophy*, p. 101.
11. *Ibid.*, p. 112.
12. *Quest for Certainty*, p. 275.
13. *Ibid.*
14. *Ibid.*
15. Schilpp (ed.), *John Dewey*, p. 589.
16. *Ibid.*, p. 587.
17. *Ibid.*, p. 590.
18. *Ibid.*, p. 588.
19. *Quest for Certainty*, pp. 273-74.
20. *Ibid.*, p. 36.

21. *Ibid.*, p. 251.
22. See Note 19.
23. *Ibid.*, pp. 86-87.
24. *Ibid.*, p. 277.
25. This problem of consequences and natural intelligence will again be considered in Chapter 5 from the standpoint of Dewey's religion, and in Chapter 7 from the standpoint of his logic.
26. *Ibid.*, p. 47.
27. "Dewey's Interpretation of Religion" in Schilpp (ed.), *John Dewey*, p. 408.
28. John Dewey and James H. Tufts, *Ethics, passim*, especially Chapters VI and VIII.
29. *Quest for Certainty*, p. 302.
30. *Ibid.*
31. *Ibid.*, p. 306.
32. *Ibid.*
33. *Ibid.*, p. 307.
34. *Ibid.*, p. 287.
35. Immanuel Kant, *The Critique of Pure Reason* (Chicago, 1952), p. 8.
36. Norman Kemp Smith, *A Commentary to Kant's 'A Critique of Pure Reason'* (New York, 1962), p. 24.
37. *Ibid.*
38. Kant, *The Critique of Pure Reason*, p. 12.
39. *Quest for Certainty*, p. 307.
40. *Ibid.*, p. 308.
41. *Ibid.*
42. *Reconstruction in Philosophy*, p. 164.
43. *Ibid.*, p. 163.
44. *Ibid.*, pp. 163-64.
45. *Ibid.*
46. *Ibid.*, p. 163.
47. *Ibid.*, pp. 163, 164.
48. *Experience and Nature*, p. 301.

Chapter Five

1. *A Common Faith* (New Haven, 1934), p. 27.
2. *Ibid.*, pp. 23-24.
3. *Ibid.*, p. 52.
4. *Ibid.*, p. 53.
5. *Ibid.*, p. 50.
6. *Ibid.*, p. 51.
7. *Ibid.*, pp. 53-54.
8. *Mind and Deity* (London, 1941), pp. 289-90.

9. *A Common Faith*, p. 54.
10. Cf. especially Chapter III of John Hick, *Philosophy of Religion* (Englewood Cliffs, N. J., 1963; and I. M. Crombie, "Philosophy and Falsification" in Antony Flew and Alasdair Macintyre (eds.), *New Essays in Philosophical Theology* (London, 1958).
11. "Nature," in C. F. Harrold and W. D. Templeman (eds.), *English Prose of the Victorian Era* (New York, 1938), pp. 737, 739.
12. *A Common Faith*, p. 55.
13. *Ibid.*, pp. 55-56.
14. *Ibid.*, p. 84.
15. *The Phenomenon of Man* (New York, 1961), p. 293.
16. *A Common Faith*, p. 53.
17. *Experience and Nature*, p. 419.
18. *A Common Faith*, pp. 70, 71.
19. *Ibid.*, pp. 71-72.
20. *Ibid.*, pp. 72-73.
21. Cf. Henry Margenau, *Thomas and the Physics of 1958: A Confrontation* (Milwaukee, 1958), p. 34.
22. *A Common Faith*, p. 77.
23. *Human Nature and Conduct*, pp. 1-2.
24. *Ibid.*, pp. 2-3.
25. *A Common Faith*, p. 79.
26. *Ibid.*, p. 80.
27. *Ibid.*, p. 84.
28. *Ibid.*
29. Manford George Gutzke, *John Dewey's Thought and Its Implications for Christian Education* (New York, 1956), *passim.*
30. Robert J. Roth, *John Dewey and Self-Realization* (Englewood Cliffs, New Jewsey, 1963), *passim.*
31. *A Common Faith*, p. 84.
32. *Ibid.*, p. 85.
33. Dewey and Tufts, *Ethics*, p. 109.

Chapter Six

1. *Experience and Nature*, p. 358.
2. *Art as Experience* (New York, 1934), p. 55.
3. *Ibid.*, p. 17.
4. Cf. Havelock Ellis, *The Dance of Life* (New York, 1923), *passim.*
5. *Art as Experience*, p. 14.
6. *Ibid.*, p. 15.
7. *Ibid.*, p. 14.
8. *Ibid.*, p. 15.
9. *Ibid.*, pp. 16, 17.

10. "Fate" in *The Complete Works of Ralph Waldo Emerson* (Boston, 1904), VI, 47-48.
11. *Art as Experience*, pp. 27-28.
12. John Blewett (ed.), *John Dewey: His Thought and Influence*, p. 6.
13. *Ibid.*, p. 20.
14. *Art as Experience*, p. 195.
15. *Ibid.*
16. *Experience and Nature*, p. 419, quoting Justice Oliver Wendell Homes, Jr.
17. *Art as Experience*, p. 19.
18. Cf. an interview with Dewey reported by Max Eastman, "John Dewey," *The Atlantic Monthly*, CLXVIII (December, 1941), 673.
19. *Art as Experience*, p. 20.
20. *Ibid.*, pp. 22-23.
21. *Ibid.*, p. 81.
22. *Ibid.*, p. 77.
23. *Ibid.*, p. 348.
24. *Ibid.*, p. 103.
25. *Ibid.*, p. 85.
26. *Ibid.*, p. 89.
27. *Ibid.*, p. 94, quoting Dr. A. C. Barnes.
28. *Ibid.*, p. 95.
29. *Ibid.*, p. 99.
30. *Ibid.*, p. 103.
31. *Ibid.*, p. 114.
32. *Ibid.*, pp. 131-32.
33. *Ibid.*, p. 133.
34. *Ibid.*, p. 349.
35. "Some Questions on Dewey's Esthetics," P. A. Schilpp (ed.), *The Philosophy of John Dewey*, p. 385.
36. *Ibid.*, p. 386.
37. *Ibid.*
38. *Ibid.*
39. *Ibid.*, pp. 551, 552.
40. *Art as Experience*, p. 347.
41. *Ibid.*, p. 151.
42. *Ibid.*, pp. 178-79.
43. *Ibid.*, p. 187.
44. *Ibid.*, p. 191.
45. *Ibid.*, p. 192.
46. *Ibid.*, p. 193.
47. *Ibid.*, pp. 193-94.
48. *Ibid.*, p. 349.
49. *Ibid.*, p. 244.

50. *Ibid.*, p. 253.
51. *Ibid.*, p. 259.
52. *Ibid.*, p. 271.
53. *Ibid.*, p. 290.
54. *Ibid.*, p. 293.
55. *Ibid.*, p. 294.
56. *Ibid.*, p. 297.
57. *Ibid.*, p. 303.
58. *Ibid.*, p. 308.
59. *Ibid.*, p. 310.
60. *Ibid.*, p. 315.
61. *Ibid.*, p. 317.
62. *Ibid.*, p. 318.
63. *Ibid.*
64. *Ibid.*
65. *Ibid.*, p. 319.
66. "A Note on the Verse of John Milton," *Essays and Studies of the English Association* (Oxford, England, 1936), XXI, 38 *et passim*.
67. *Art as Experience*, p. 321.
68. *Ibid.*
69. *Ibid.*, p. 322.
70. *Experience and Nature*, pp. 421-22.
71. *Art as Experience*, p. 322.
72. *Ibid.*, p. 334.
73. Schilpp (ed.), *The Philosophy of John Dewey*, p. 543.
74. *Art as Experience*, p. 335.
75. *Ibid.*, p. 348.
76. *Ibid.*, pp. 338-39.
77. *Ibid.*, p. 349.
78. *Experience and Nature*, p. 358.
79. *Art as Experience*, p. 339.

Chapter Seven

1. *Logic: The Theory of Inquiry* (New York, 1938).
2. *The Influence of Darwin on Philosophy* (New York, 1910), p. 13.
3. *Logic: The Theory of Inquiry*, p. 19.
4. *Ibid.*, p. 24.
5. *The Influence of Darwin on Philosophy*, p. 14.
6. Charles Darwin, *The Origin of Species and the Descent of Man* (New York, n.d.), p. 374.
7. *Logic: The Theory of Inquiry*, p. 23.
8. *Ibid.*, p. 24.
9. *Ibid.*, p. 25.
10. *The Quest for Being* (New York, 1963), *passim*.

Notes and References

11. *Logic: The Theory of Inquiry*, p. 25.
12. *Ibid.*, p. 43.
13. *Ibid.*, pp. 43-44.
14. Cf. the following statement by Jacques Maritain:
"John Dewey's effort can be considered as one of the most significant made by modern philosophical thought toward the achievement of an integral or absolute naturalism. We may add that by virtue of this very fact it was one of the efforts of thought most typically subject to a radical ambiguity.

"This radical ambiguity shows itself in a perpetual, and equivocal, alternation between 'nature' as the object of the investigations of science (in the modern or empiriological sense of this word)—in this use the word 'nature' carries a completely phenomenal connotation—and 'Nature' as a philosophical entity, with a value all the more prized by a thinker like Dewey because in his passionate desire to arrive at a total organic unification of the field of knowledge he posited Nature to replace Spirit as an antithesis and antidote of Spirit. . . .

"On the one hand, the rejection of the absolute is at the very root of every philosophy which wants to be totally naturalist. On the other hand, it is impossible to be totally naturalistic without enclosing universal reality in a giant all-embracing Nature, that is, in an absolutized Nature. . . ."
(*Moral Philosophy* [New York, 1964], pp. 401, 402.)

15. *Logic: The Theory of Inquiry*, p. 25.
16. *Ibid.*, p. 44.
17. *Ibid.*, p. 58.
18. *Great Books of the Western World* (Chicago, 1952), LIII, 897.
19. *The Torch of Life* (New York, 1962), p. 79.
20. *Ibid.*, pp. 79-80.
21. *Logic: The Theory of Inquiry*, p. 58.
22. *Ibid.*
23. *The Phenomenon of Man* (New York, 1961)—hereafter referred to as *Phenomenon*.
24. *Ibid.*, 289.
25. *Ibid.*, p. 56.
26. *Ibid.*, p. 57, quoting Haldane.
27. Huxley, Introduction, Chardin, *Phenomenon*, p. 19.
28. *Ibid.*
29. *Ibid.*, p. 20.
30. *Ibid.*
31. *Logic: The Theory of Inquiry*, p. 93.
32. Robert J. Roth, *Dewey and Self-Realization* (Englewood Cliffs, New Jersey, 1962), p. 126.
33. George R. Geiger, *John Dewey in Perspective* (New York, 1958), passim.

34. Max Eastman, "John Dewey," *The Atlantic Monthly*, CLXVIII (December, 1941), 673.

35. Roth, *Dewey*, p. 139.

36. *Logic: The Theory of Inquiry*, p. 198.

37. *Ibid.*, p. 67.

38. J. H. Bernard (ed.), *Kant's Critique of Judgment* (London, 1931), p. 326.

39. Cf., for example, the argument in Edward L. Schaub, "Dewey's Interpretation of Religion," in P. A. Schilpp (ed.), *The Philosophy of John Dewey*, pp. 408-10.

40. *Logic: The Theory of Inquiry*, p. 77.

41. Letter to H. G. Wells, 1906, quoted in George Seldes (ed.), *The Great Quotations* (New York, 1960), p. 359.

42. Dewey himself in one place acknowledged that he may have over-stressed consequences. See his statement in Schilpp (ed.), *John Dewey*, p. 591.

43. *Logic: The Theory of Inquiry*, p. 175.

44. *Experience and Nature* (New York, 1925), p. 78.

45. *Art as Experience* (New York, 1934), p. 25.

46. Introduction to Melvin Rader (ed.), *A Modern Book of Esthetics* (New York, 1952), p. xxxi.

47. This attempt to combine opposites, even though these be the Romantic and the Classical, is here called Romantic because it tries, in Romantic fashion, to do what is impossible. It will be noted that the claim is not an alternation between the Apollonian and the Dionysian but the coexistence and the synthesis of these two opposites in the same person at the same time.

48. Dewey in Schilpp (ed.), *John Dewey*, p. 543.

49. *Logic: The Theory of Inquiry*, p. 416.

50. *Ibid.*, p. 456.

51. *Ibid.*, p. 422.

52. *Ibid.*, p. 467.

53. *Ibid.*, p. 497.

54. Dewey in Schilpp (ed.), *John Dewey*, p. 572.

55. *Ibid.*

56. *Logic: The Theory of Inquiry*, p. 508.

57. *Ibid.*, p. 111.

58. Dewey in Schilpp (ed.), *John Dewey*, p. 573.

59. Miss Jane Dewey in *ibid.*, pp. 42-43.

60. Sidney Hook, *John Dewey* (New York, 1939), p. 101.

61. *Ibid.*

62. *Ibid.*

63. As I demonstrate in Chapter 8, Dewey considerably distorts Peirce's philosophy by almost completely ignoring what Peirce considered to be the

most important implications of his pragmaticism. For example, Peirce says again and again that his pragmaticism points to a transcendent God, especially in the "Neglected Argument," which he calls "the First State of a scientific inquiry, resulting in a hypothesis of God's Reality of the very highest plausibility, whose ultimate test must lie in its value in the self-controlled growth of man's conduct of life . . ." (*Collected Papers of Charles Sanders Peirce*, Cambridge, Massachusetts, 1958, VI, 327-28, *et passim*). It should be clear from this argument that Peirce would have disapproved of this naturalistic application of his philosophy made by Hook.

64. Hook, *John Dewey*, p. 99.
65. *Ibid.*
66. *Ibid.*
67. *Logic: The Theory of Inquiry*, p. 535.

Chapter Eight

1. Dewey in Schilpp (ed.), *John Dewey*, p. 494.
2. Letter quoted in Ralph Barton Perry, *The Thought and Character of William James* (Boston, 1936), II, 532—hereafter referred to as Perry, *William James*.
3. James, *A Pluralistic Universe* (New York, 1932), pp. 310-11, 309, 310, 308.
4. Perry, *William James*, II, 533.
5. Rudolf Carnap in P. A. Schilpp (ed.), *The Philosophy of Rudolf Carnap* (LaSalle, Illinois, 1963), p. 868—hereafter referred to as Schilpp (ed.), *Carnap*. (Although this book appeared eleven years after Dewey's death, the quotations from and about Carnap—indicating the rather extensive similarity between his views and those of Dewey—refer to views which Carnap says that he and most other logical empiricists held and expressed at, in some cases even before, the time when Dewey was attacking them so sharply.)
6. Cf. especially the laborious attacks made by Dewey and Bentley against the "vague logic" of logical empiricists such as Carnap, C. W. Morris, and others—John Dewey and Arthur Bentley, *Knowing and the Known* (Boston, 1949), *passim*.
7. Carnap in Schilpp (ed.), *Carnap*, pp. 865-66.
8. *Ibid.*, pp. 866, 867.
9. *Ibid.*, p. 867.
10. *Ibid.*, 868-69.
11. Dewey and Bentley, *Knowing and the Known*, pp. 38-39.
12. Carnap in Schilpp (ed.), *Carnap*, p. 883.
13. *Ibid.*, p. 863.
14. Hans Reichenbach, "Dewey's Theory of Science," in Schilpp (ed.), *John Dewey*, p. 178.

15. Kaplan in Schilpp (ed.), *Carnap*, pp. 844, 847, 853-54.

16. Dewey, "Peirce's Theory of Linguistic Signs, Thought, and Meaning," *The Journal of Philosophy*, XLIII (February 14, 1946), 86.

17. Letter in *Journal of Philosophy*, XLIII (June 20, 1946), 363-64.

18. *Collected Papers of Charles Sanders Peirce* (Cambridge, Massachusetts, 1958), VIII, 182—hereafter referred to as *Collected Papers of Peirce*.

19. *Ibid.*, pp. 145-47.

20. "Editorial Note," *Collected Papers of Peirce*, VI, v.

21. *Collected Papers of Peirce*, VI, 335.

22. "Religion and Theology in Peirce," in Philip P. Wiener and Frederic H. Young (eds.), *Studies in the Philosophy of Charles Peirce* (Cambridge, Massachusetts, 1952), p. 251—hereafter referred to as Wiener and Young (eds.), *Peirce*.

23. *Colected Papers of Peirce*, VI, 327-28.

24. *Ibid.*, pp. 312, 313.

25. *Collected Papers of Peirce*, V, 270.

26. *Collected Papers of Peirce*, VI, 312-13.

27. *Ibid.*, pp. 314, 316, 317.   This line of reasoning is similar to that of Cardinal Newman in his *A Grammar of Assent*. According to Newman, the extended operation of "the Illative Sense" will adduce "converging probabilities" that will bring the mind to a state of certitude (as contrasted with certainty, a quality of propositions) concerning the existence of God—*A Grammar of Assent* (New York, 1947), pp. 244, 262.

28. *Collected Papers of Peirce*, pp. 327-28, 331, 332.

29. Dewey, "The Pragmatism of Peirce," in M. R. Cohen (ed.), Charles S. Peirce, *Chance, Love, and Logic* (New York, 1949), p. 308.

30. Cf. again Peirce's statement, quoted above, that "the N. A. Neglected Argument is the First State of a scientific inquiry, resulting in a hypothesis [of God's Reality] of the very highest Plausibility, whose ultimate test must lie in its value in the self-controlled growth of man's conduct of life. . . ."

31. Dewey, "The Pragmatism of Peirce," p. 304.

32. *Ibid.*, pp. 306-7.

33. Cf. Note 30 and same quotation in text above.

34. *Quest for Being*, p. 199.

35. *Ibid.*, p. 101.

36. *Collected Papers of Peirce*, VI, 110-11.

37. *The Journal of Philosophy*, XXXII (December 19, 1935), pp. 701, 707, 708.

38. *Collected Papers of Peirce*, VI, 335.

39. *Collected Papers of Peirce*, I, 187.

40. *Ibid.*, p. 26.

41. Wiener in Wiener and Young (eds.), *Peirce*, p. 148.

42. *Collected Papers of Peirce*, VI, 118.

43. Wiener in Wiener and Young (eds.), *Peirce*, p. 148.

44. *Collected Papers of Peirce*, VI, 117.

45. *Ibid.*, pp. 117-18.

46. *Ibid.*, pp. 43-44.

47. *Chance, Love, and Logic*, pp. 284-85.

48. *Ibid.*, p. 287.

49. *Collected Papers of Peirce*, VI, 327-28.

50. *Ibid.*, p. 86.

51. *Ibid.*, pp. 20-21.

52. (Indeed, as we have said before, Darwin's concluding sentence in his *Origin of Species*, reinforced by a later statement in his *Autobiography*, indicates that at the time when he wrote the *Origin* he himself so interpreted it, although he later became an agnostic.)

53. "Evolutionary Love" in *Chance, Love, and Logic*, pp. 284-85, 287.

54. *Experience and Nature*, p. 255.

55. *Ibid.*, pp. 421-22.

56. *The Phenomenon of Man*, pp. 55ff.

57. *Ibid.*, p. 59.

58. Cf. Peirce's reference (*Chance, Love, and Logic*, p. 253) to "the excessively complicated constitution of the protoplasm molecule."

59. *The Phenomenon of Man*, pp. 60-61.

60. *Ibid.*, p. 72.

61. *Ibid.*, p. 74.

62. *Ibid.*, p. 29.

63. *Collected Papers of Peirce*, II, 168.

64. *The Phenomenon of Man*, p. 258.

65. *Ibid.*, pp. 259-60.

66. *Ibid.*, p. 294.

67. *Quest for Being*, pp. 96-97.

68. Henry Margenau, *Thomas and the Physics of 1958: A Confrontation* (Milwaukee, 1958), pp. 34, 35, 36.

69. "On the Significance of Science for Religious Thought" (Division of Higher Education, The Board of Education of the Methodist Church, 1964), pp. 4, 14.

70. *Philosophic Problems of Nuclear Science* (New York, 1952), p. 93.

71. *Ibid.*, p. 119.

72. *Quest for Being*, p. 127.

73. *Philosophic Problems of Nuclear Science*, pp. 118-19.

74. *Existentialism—For and Against* (Cambridge, England, 1964), p. 2.

75. *Quest for Being*, p. 194.

76. *Symbolism and Belief*, pp. 371, 372, 376-77.

77. Richard Niebuhr, *Radical Monotheism and Western Culture* (New York, 1960), p. 89.

78. *Reconstruction in Philosophy*, p. 59.

79. George R. Geiger, *John Dewey in Perspective*, p. 225.
80. *Experience and Nature*, pp. 421-22.
81. *The Mystery of Being* (Chicago, 1950), I, 211-12 *et passim.*
82. Roubiczek, *Existentialism: For and Against*, p. 2.
83. *Philosophic Problems of Nuclear Science*, p. 119.
84. *Pensées* (New York, 1941), No. 267, p. 93.
85. *Ibid.*, No. 273, p. 94.
86. *Ibid.*, No. 282, p. 95.

Chapter Nine

1. Richard J. Bernstein, "Introduction," Richard J. Bernstein (ed.), John Dewey, *On Experience, Nature, and Freedom*, p. xxvi.
2. Dewey in Schilpp (ed.), *John Dewey*, p. 543.
3. Warner Berthoff, *American Realism* (New York, 1965), pp. 172-73.
4. Werner Heisenberg, *Philosophical Problems of Nuclear Science*, p. 99.

Selected Bibliography

PRIMARY SOURCES

(For best and most comprehensive bibliography see M. H. Thomas [ed.], *John Dewey: A Centennial Bibliography* [Chicago: The University of Chicago Press, 1962])

The School and Society. Chicago: The University of Chicago Press, 1899. Revised edition, 1915.

Studies in Logical Theory. Chicago: The University of Chicago Press, 1903.

Ethics (with James H. Tufts). New York: Henry Holt and Company, 1908. Revised edition, 1932.

How We Think. Boston: D. C. Heath & Co., 1910. Revised edition, 1933.

The Influence of Darwin on Philosophy. New York: Henry Holt and Company, 1910.

Democracy and Education. New York: The Macmillan Company, 1916.

Essays in Experimental Logic. Chicago: The University of Chicago Press, 1916.

Reconstruction in Philosophy. New York: Henry Holt and Company, 1920. Enlarged edition, Boston: The Beacon Press, 1948; New York: The New American Library, 1950.

Human Nature and Conduct. New York: Henry Holt and Company, 1922. Modern Library edition, 1930.

Experience and Nature. Chicago, London: Open Court Publishing Company, 1925. Revised edition, New York: W. W. Norton & Co., 1929.

The Public and Its Problems. New York: Henry Holt and Company, 1927.

Characters and Events (edited by Joseph Ratner). New York: Henry Holt and Company, 1929. Two volumes.

The Quest for Certainty. New York: Minton, Balch & Co., 1929.

Individualism, Old and New. New York: Minton, Balch & Co., 1930.

Philosophy and Civilization. New York: Minton, Balch & Co., 1931.

Art as Experience. New York: Minton, Balch & Co., 1934.

A Common Faith. New Haven: Yale University Press, 1934.

Liberalism and Social Action. New York: G. P. Putnam's Sons, 1935.

Logic: The Theory of Inquiry. New York: Henry Holt and Company, 1938.

Freedom and Culture. New York: G. P. Putnam's Sons, 1939.

Problems of Men. New York: Philosophical Library, 1946.

Knowing and the Known (with Arthur F. Bentley). Boston: The Beacon Press, 1949.

SECONDARY SOURCES

BERNSTEIN, RICHARD J., ed. Introduction. *John Dewey: On Experience, Nature, and Freedom.* New York: The Liberal Arts Press, 1960. Carefully organized essay presenting Dewey's development as divided into three "different though continuous stages" which are marked by "fundamental shifts of emphases." Bernstein, with only partial success, defends Dewey against various forms of attack. All of these he calls "the popular confusion which makes up the Dewey legend."

BLEWETT, JOHN, ed. *John Dewey: His Thought and Influence.* New York: Fordham University Press, 1960. Stimulating series of essays by Roman Catholic theologians and philosophers. Thoroughly scholarly but very lively in pointing out the defects of Dewey's naturalism.

COHEN, MORRIS R. "John Dewey and His School." *American Thought*: A *Critical Sketch.* Glencoe, Illinois: The Free Press, 1954, pp. 290-303. Surprisingly sharp attack against Dewey by one, who though himself an agnostic, believes that "no philosophy that lacks a cosmic outlook can hope to do full justice to the specifically human problem." Somewhat inaccurate in maintaining that Dewey demands "discontinuance of all worship." As *A Common Faith* demonstrates, Dewey would certainly have agreed with Cohen's insistence that "we ought to look for new objects more worthy of human adoration."

GEIGER, GEORGE R. *John Dewey in Perspective.* New York: Oxford University Press, 1958. A study by a devoted follower who defends and echoes Dewey, insisting that "the Deweyan naturalism being recommended here" is not "the 'old-fashioned' kind—that of reductionism and 'nothing but.' . . ." Therefore, Geiger can prophesy with the master that "uniting nature and cementing the union with the method of free intelligence can bring a new vision which poets, and even mystics, will learn to celebrate" (227-28).

GUTZKE, MANFORD GEORGE. *John Dewey's Thought and Its Implication for Christian Education.* New York: Columbia University Press, 1956. Maintains that the "scientific method is applicable in the field of religious phenomena" and that this procedure is implicit in Dewey's philosophy. Maintains also that Dewey's version of the scientific method may be used to great advantage in the service of the Christian religion and that the validity of such a procedure is implicit in Dewey's philosophy. Gutzke's thesis could be successfully maintained only if it referred to Dewey's religion of science and nature instead of the Christian religion with its transcendent God.

HENDEL, CHARLES W. ed. *Dewey and the Experimental Spirit in Philosophy.* New York: The Liberal Arts Press, 1959. Contains four essays, three of which merely explain, without challenging any part of, Dewey's form of experimental empiricism. The last essay, by Professor John E. Smith,

Selected Bibliography

while predominantly sympathetic, finds Dewey's philosophy inadequate in developing a satisfactory theory of personality and in acknowledging only specific problems and the instrumental response.

HOOK, SIDNEY. *John Dewey: An Intellectual Portrait*. New York: The John Day Company, 1939. A study by a philosopher who is perhaps the most devoted of all Dewey's disciples, who says that "as the philosopher of American democracy John Dewey has been able to capture the imagination and allegiance of thousands of people who have only a dim idea of technical achievements" (232). Hook's only objection (and this a mild one), repeated in more detail, in his *The Quest for Being* (New York: The Dell Publishing Company, 1961), is that Dewey's approval of using the term *God*, even though limited to an imaginative projection of man's own ideals, may easily be misinterpreted by traditional theists.

LAWSON, DOUGLAS E., and ARTHUR E. LEAN (eds.). *John Dewey and the World View*. Carbondale: Southern Illinois University Press, 1964. Five essays (four treating Dewey's educational philosophy and one his "world view") which give useful summaries of Dewey's ideas and influence but are undiscriminating in their almost completely unqualified praise of his philosophy.

MARITAIN, JACQUES. "John Dewey and the Objectivity of Values—the Inconsistency of Absolute Naturalism." *Moral Philosophy*. New York: Charles Scribner's Sons, 1964. Devastating analysis of Dewey's philosophy from the neo-Thomist point of view. Especially convincing in explaining the inadequacy of an ethics (like that of Dewey) regulated exclusively by the positive sciences or the sciences of phenomena. Guidance from these sciences, says Maritain, "involves only a kind of *premorality*, and only acquires authentically ethical significance if it is regulated and controlled from a higher level by the aid of criteria concerned with the conscience proper" (412-13).

NATHANSON, JEROME. *John Dewey: The Reconstruction of the Democratic Life*. New York: Scribner's, 1951. Exalts Dewey for teaching us how to "free the possibilities in human nature" (18)—how to "climb the peaks from which we get an endless vista of endless possibilities" (119). Typical of the Dewey cult, which contains a number of significant parallels with the Emerson cult of the nineteenth century.

RATNER, JOSEPH, ed. Introduction. *Intelligence in the Modern World: John Dewey's Philosophy*. New York: The Modern Library—Random House, 1939. Analyzes the attitude of Dewey and several of his contemporaries—especially Russell, Whitehead, and Einstein—toward the scientific method as exhibited in both scientific theory and laboratory experimentation. Although admitting that Dewey occasionally has lapses in following the scientific method, this study exalts him as one of the great philosophers of all time because almost always he "employed controlled inquiry—or the method of intelligence—in the fields

of philosophy and the social sciences, and all human affairs . . ."
(241).

ROTH, ROBERT J. *John Dewey and Self-Realization*. Englewood Cliffs, N.J.: Prentice-Hall, 1962. A sympathetic study by a Catholic scholar, who (a little too generously) says that "though Dewey may have explicitly eliminated the transcendental, his notion of community, 'sense of wholeness' and 'onward thrust' are open to it and provide a starting point for anyone who would wish to extend further his insights" (144).

SCHILPP, PAUL A., ed. *The Philosophy of John Dewey*. New York: Tudor Publishing Company, 1951. Valuable volume in The Library of Living Philosophers containing a short biography by Dewey's daughters, critical essays by seventeen philosophers, and Dewey's lengthy comments, most of which are devoted to answering adverse criticism. Most of the essays are written by naturalists and are predominantly favorable though there are many objections to minor points.

WHITE, MORTON. *The Origin of Dewey's Instrumentalism*. New York: Columbia University Press, 1943. Most thorough study of the early Dewey, including influences on him and his gradual abandonment of Hegelianism in favor of instrumentalism or, as Dewey preferred to call it, experimental empiricism.

Index

Index

Hook, Sidney, 26, 97-98, 109-10, 120, 127, 129-30, 132
Hospers, John, 88-89
Huxley, Sir Julian, 101-2

Isaiah, 93

James, William 15, 17, 23, 36, 53, 99-100; 106, 111-13
Jeans, James, 129
Jefferson, Thomas, 76
John the Baptist, 92

Kant, Emmanuel, 15, 38-39, 59, 65-66, 84, 105, 117, 119, 123, 138; Kantian, 22, 87
Kaplan, Abraham, 115
Keats, John, 82, 84, 85, 92
Khayyam, Omar, 46
Kierkegaard, Sören, 119

Laird, John, 72
Langer, Susanne, 48, 99
Lotze, Rudolf, 29

Marcel, Gabriel, 132-33
Margenau, Henry, 128-29
Maritain, Jacques, 30
Middle Ages, 21, 106
Mill, John Stuart, 73
Milton, John, 89
Morris, Charles W., 111, 115-16
Morris, George Sylvester, 14

Newtonian, 65
Niebuhr, Richard, 131-32
Nietzschean, 127

Parker, Dewitt, 87-88
Parodi, Dominique, 108
Pascal, Blaise, 131, 133
Pater, Walter, 106
Peirce, Charles Sanders, 14, 110, 111, 113, 115-25, 127, 130
Pepper, Stephen, 84-86; 88
Pestalozzi, Johann Heinrich, 135

Plato, 39, 87, 90; Platonic philosophy, 38, 104
Ptolemaic system, 65

Raby, Sister Joseph Mary, 32-33
Rader, Melvin, 107
Randall, John Herman, 37
Reichenbach, Hans, 40-41, 91, 115, 136-37
Renaissance, 21-22
Richards, I. A., 70
Roth, Robert J., 103
Roubiczek, Paul, 130, 133
Rousseau, Jean Jacques, 135; Rousseauism, 76
Royce, Josiah, 45
Russell, Bertrand, 39, 48, 113-14, 136

St. Paul, 73-74, 102
St. Thomas, 39
St. Thomas Aquinas, 39, 75, 81, 128
Santayana, George, 37, 39, 81, 89-90, 136
Saul of Tarsus, 21
Schaub, Edward L., 63
Schelling, Friedrich von, 120
Schilling, Harold K., 128-29, 130
Schilpp, Paul Arthur, 40, 60-61, 67
Shakespeare, William, 89-90
Shelley, Percy Bysshe, 82, 84, 92
Smith, John E., 117
Smith, Norman Kemp, 65
Spinoza, Baruch, 14, 26, 39
Stevenson, Charles, 115
Stuart, Henry W., 60

Torrey, H. A. P., 13
Trotsky, Leon, 18-19

White, Morton, 16, 28-29
Whitehead, Alfred North, 27, 49
Whitman, Walt, 27, 71, 103
Wiener, Philip, 122-23
Wilson, Edmund, 137
Wolf, Lucy Brandauer (daughter), 19
Wordsworth, William 27, 68, 71, 83, 84, 103
World War I, 58, 75